D1314559

1st EDITION

Perspectives on Diseases and Disorders

Phobias

Other books in this series:

AIDS
Alzheimer's Disease
Autism
Cancer
Diabetes
Down Syndrome
Heart Disease
Obesity

1st EDITION

Perspectives on Diseases and Disorders

Phobias

Tom and Gena Metcalf
Book Editors

GALE
CENGAGE Learning

Detroit • New York • San Francisco • New Haven, Conn • Waterville, Maine • London

Christine Nasso, *Publisher*
Elizabeth Des Chenes, *Managing Editor*

Articles in Greenhaven Press anthologies are often edited for length to meet page
requirements. In addition, original titles of these works are changed to clearly present
the main thesis and to explicitly indicate the author's opinion. Every effort is made to
ensure that Greenhaven Press accurately reflects the original intent of the authors.
Every effort has been made to trace the owners of copyrighted material.

Cover: Image copyright Robynrg, 2007. Used under license of Shutterstock.com.

LIBRARY OF CONGRESS CATALOGING-IN-PUBLICATION DATA

Phobias / Tom and Gena Metcalf, book editor[s].
    p. cm. — (Perspectives on diseases and disorders)
    Includes bibliographical references and index.
    ISBN-13: 978-0-7377-4027-1 (hardcover)
    1. Phobias. I. Metcalf, Tom. II. Metcalf, Gena.
    RC535.P485 2008
    616.85'225—dc22

                                                    2008017918

Printed in the United States of America
    3 4 5 6 7 12 11 10 09

CONTENTS

INTRODUCTION

Fear is a normal emotion. When confronted with a threat or unfamiliar situation, fear and the physiological responses it triggers are completely expected. Pounding heart, headaches, goose bumps, dry mouth, and knots in the stomach—these are symptoms that all of us have experienced at one time or another. All of these reactions are normal responses to stressful situations; all are related to the primal "fight-or-flight syndrome" that helped our distant ancestors through many crises. Once, these responses to fear had specific benefits; today for many of us they pose drawbacks.

A Historical Basis for Fear

Our forebears lived a more dangerous lifestyle than we do today and were braced for the challenges they faced. We, however, are genetically programmed by their defense mechanisms; our physical and psychological reactions are designed to protect us from a life we no longer live. The racing heartbeat pumped more oxygen to fuel muscles, enabling our ancestors to face an enemy or to run from him. The headaches were the result of a thyroid hormone rush that gave them the physical boost to face a saber-toothed tiger. Goosebumps and sweat heightened sensory perception; skin pallor occurred as blood was diverted to muscles. Dry mouth and knots in the stomach occurred because the digestive tract shut down in order to divert more energy to the extremities. All of these reactions were great in another era, but do they have a place in our world today? The physiological responses that saved our Paleolithic ancestors have a limited role for most of us in daily life. Certainly for a soldier in combat these responses are beneficial. So, too, for a person who hears a burglar in the middle of the night or a jogger who is confronted with a predator. But what happens when the signals go awry?

People with phobias experience these symptoms and more. What triggers a phobia is not easy to pinpoint. Some may be traced to a traumatic event. Being bitten by a spider might trigger arachnophobia. Evidence suggests that predisposition to phobic behavior may be hereditary, as some phobias seem to run in families. Gender plays a role, too, as women are twice as likely to develop a phobia than are men.

Many people with specific phobias live quite normal lives simply by avoiding the object or event that triggers the phobic reaction. A recent Gallup poll, for example, revealed that 51 percent of Americans are afraid of snakes. This does not pose a significant problem for most people

The physiological responses caused by fear helped our Paleolithic ancestors survive a dangerous world. **(Peter V. Bianchi/ National Geographic/ Getty Images)**

since the vast majority of us have no contact with them. Whether the fear is normal or phobic is academic in these cases. But when a phobia interferes with one's life, then it becomes a problem.

Social Phobia

Specific or simple phobias are the easiest to overcome. Other phobias are more pervasive and defy simple treatment. Social phobia, the fear of embarrassing oneself in public, and agoraphobia, the fear of a panic attack in public, are more severe and pose serious limitations on the lives of those who experience them. Many people with specific phobias live relatively normal lives; those suffering from social phobia or agoraphobia, on the other hand, are crippled in almost every aspect of theirs.

Social phobias typically appear in childhood or adolescence. Phobias occurring at this stage in development can be psychologically crippling, since this is the period of development when a person is building personal and social skills. This is also a period when the social pressure to conform is strong. Symptoms for social phobia include an overwhelming uneasiness and fear of humiliation in the presence of strangers. The anxiety experienced may cause people with social phobias to avoid social events; they may panic with the prospect of a job interview. Social phobias can come and go depending on the circumstances of a person's life. A person who experiences social phobia as a young adult may see it wane when he or she marries, only to have it reappear with a divorce or death of a partner.

Agoraphobia

Agoraphobia is another devastating phobia. More serious than social phobia and specific phobias, agoraphobia is the fear of being in a place where one cannot escape or get help. The onset of agoraphobia frequently begins with a panic attack. Whether alone in a car or walking through a mall, the victim is overcome with fear and experiences a variety of frightening symptoms. Sometimes chest pains are so severe the victim thinks he is having a heart attack. These symptoms cause the victim to avoid the location or circumstance where the panic attack occurred. Each recurrence of a panic attack reinforces the fear of having another. Over time the anticipatory anxiety can become so great that it cripples a person's life. People suffering from agoraphobia are frequently so overwhelmed that they fear leaving their homes or neighborhood. Sometimes the agoraphobic can venture out with a "safe" person, but this dependency does not help to address the problem. Agoraphobia carries fear of losing control or having a panic attack in a public place, fear of traveling alone, fear of confined places where escape may be difficult, fear of crowded places. Symptoms include upset stomach, rapid heart beat, heavy perspiration, chest pain, a sense of losing

Fifty-one percent of Americans are afraid of snakes. (Peter Charlesworth/On Asia/ Jupiterimages)

control, and trouble breathing. Agoraphobia has so many aspects that the World Health Organization considers it to be a cluster of interrelated phobias.

Estimates of the number of sufferers vary between 3 and 5 percent of the population. As with many of the other phobias, the exact causes are unknown, but risk factors include a stressful lifestyle, a tendency toward anxiety, alcohol and substance abuse, and having other anxiety disorders. The conditions frequently appear in people in their early twenties. There is no known way to prevent agoraphobia; nevertheless, there are treatments that offer relief.

Diagnosis Is Difficult

The medical community estimates that only 9 percent of the population suffer from specific phobias and only 7 percent suffer from social phobia. Polls such as this mask the question—when does a normal fear or anxiety cross the line and become a phobia? In a multicultural world it is apparent that some cultures exhibit self-effacing behavior that could be diagnosed as social phobia by mainstream American medicine. Indeed, there are some in the medical profession that question whether doctors are overdiagnosing the condition. Some in the psychiatric profession believe that patients are being misdiagnosed; extreme shyness may not require a regimen of SSRI's and intensive behavioral therapy. Rather, the criterion for diagnosing social phobia should be the extent of the shyness. If a patient's ability to function is damaged to the extent that he or she cannot perform necessary life activities, then intervention is appropriate. Many patients, they say, do not meet this standard. Just as treatments are evolving, so too, it seems, are the standards for diagnosing conditions. Advances in therapy and medicine have demonstrated that the majority of those living with phobias can overcome their conditions and live normal, productive, and fulfilling lives.

CHAPTER 1

Understanding Phobias

Symptoms, Causes, and Treatments of Phobias

Carol A. Turkington and Rebecca J. Frey

Carol A. Turkington is the author of numerous articles about medical topics. Her coauthor, Rebecca J. Frey, is also a medical writer and is the editor of the *Encyclopedia of Cancer*. In this selection the authors discuss the different types of phobias, their causes and symptoms, and their treatment. They describe specific phobias, which affect one out of ten Americans. They discuss the differences between social phobia and shyness. They examine agoraphobia, the fear of being trapped and having a panic attack in a public place. They note that while some phobias seem to run in families, they are frequently triggered by stressful events. Phobias are highly treatable, the authors say, with medication and a variety of therapeutic treatments.

A phobia is an intense but unrealistic fear that can interfere with the ability to socialize, work, or go about everyday life, brought on by an object, event or situation.

Photo on facing page. Jimmy Stewart played a man with a fear of heights in the classic 1958 film Vertigo. (Paramount/The Kobal Collection)

SOURCE: Carol A. Turkington and Rebecca J. Frey, Ph.D., *Gale Encyclopedia of Medicine*. Belmont, CA: Gale, 2006. Copyright © 2006 Gale, a part of Cengage Learning. Reproduced by permission of Gale, a part of Cengage Learning.

Phobias Are Irrational Fears

Just about everyone is afraid of something—an upcoming job interview or being alone outside after dark. But about 18% of all Americans are tormented by irrational fears that interfere with their daily lives. They are not "crazy"—they know full well their fears are unreasonable—but they cannot control the fear. These people have phobias.

Phobias belong to a large group of mental problems known as anxiety disorders that include obsessive-compulsive disorder (OCD), panic disorder, and post-traumatic stress disorder. Phobias themselves can be divided into three specific types:

- specific phobias (formerly called "simple phobias")
- social phobia
- agoraphobia

Specific phobias. As its name suggests, a specific phobia is the fear of a particular situation or object, including anything from airplane travel to dentists. Found in one out of every 10 Americans, specific phobias seem to run in families and are roughly twice as likely to appear in women. If the person rarely encounters the feared object, the phobia does not cause much harm. However, if the feared object or situation is common, it can seriously disrupt everyday life. Common examples of specific phobias, which can begin at any age, include fear of snakes, flying, dogs, escalators, elevators, high places, or open spaces.

Social phobia. People with social phobia have deep fears of being watched or judged by others and being embarrassed in public. This may extend to a general fear of social situations—or be more specific or circumscribed, such as a fear of giving speeches or of performing (stage fright). More rarely, people with social phobia may have trouble using a public restroom, eating in a restaurant, or signing their name in front of others.

Holiday shoppers ride the escalator at a Virginia mall. Fear of escalators is a common phobia. (Joe Raedle/Getty Images)

Social phobia is not the same as shyness. Shy people may feel uncomfortable with others, but they don't experience severe anxiety, they don't worry excessively about social situations beforehand, and they don't avoid events that make them feel self-conscious. On the other hand, people with social phobia may not be shy—they may feel perfectly comfortable with people except in specific situations. Social phobias may be only mildly irritating, or they may significantly interfere with daily life. It is not unusual for people with social phobia to turn down job offers or avoid relationships because of their fears.

Agoraphobia. Agoraphobia is the intense fear of feeling trapped and having a panic attack in a public place. It usually begins between ages 15 and 35, and affects three times as many women as men—about 3% of the population.

An episode of spontaneous panic is usually the initial trigger for the development of agoraphobia. After an initial panic attack, the person becomes afraid of experiencing a second one. Patients literally "fear the fear," and worry incessantly about when and where the next attack may occur. As they begin to avoid the places or situations in which the panic attack occurred, their fear generalizes. Eventually the person completely avoids public places. In severe cases, people with agoraphobia can no longer leave their homes for fear of experiencing a panic attack.

The Causes of Phobias Are Not Clear

Experts don't really know why phobias develop, although research suggests the tendency to develop phobias may be a complex interaction between heredity and environment. Some hypersensitive people have unique chemical reactions in the brain that cause them to respond much more strongly to stress. These people also may be especially sensitive to caffeine, which triggers certain brain chemical responses.

Advances in neuroimaging have also led researchers to identify certain parts of the brain and specific neural pathways that are associated with phobias. One part of the brain that is currently being studied is the amygdala, an almond-shaped body of nerve cells involved in normal fear conditioning. Another area of the brain that appears to be linked to phobias is the posterior cerebellum.

While experts believe the tendency to develop phobias runs in families and may be hereditary, a specific stressful event usually triggers the development of a specific phobia or agoraphobia. For example, someone predisposed to develop phobias who experiences severe turbulence during a flight might go on to develop a phobia about flying. What scientists don't understand is why some people who experience a frightening or stressful event develop a phobia and others do not.

Social phobia typically appears in childhood or adolescence, sometimes following an upsetting or humiliating experience. Certain vulnerable children who have had

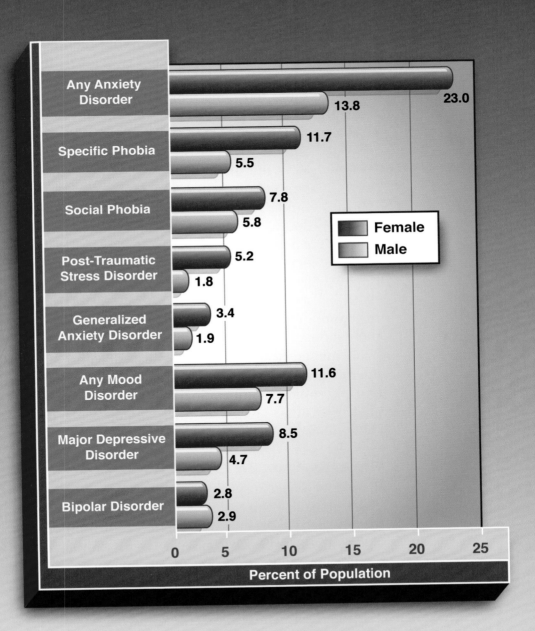

Mental Disorders Among Adults Aged 18 and Older in the Past Year, by Sex, 2001–2003

Any Anxiety Disorder
- Female: 23.0
- Male: 13.8

Specific Phobia
- Female: 11.7
- Male: 5.5

Social Phobia
- Female: 7.8
- Male: 5.8

Post-Traumatic Stress Disorder
- Female: 5.2
- Male: 1.8

Generalized Anxiety Disorder
- Female: 3.4
- Male: 1.9

Any Mood Disorder
- Female: 11.6
- Male: 7.7

Major Depressive Disorder
- Female: 8.5
- Male: 4.7

Bipolar Disorder
- Female: 2.8
- Male: 2.9

Legend: ■ Female ■ Male

X-axis: 0, 5, 10, 15, 20, 25 — **Percent of Population**

Taken from: National Comorbidity Survey Replication (NCS-R).

unpleasant social experiences (such as being rejected) or who have poor social skills may develop social phobias. The condition also may be related to low self-esteem, unassertive personality, and feelings of inferiority.

A person with agoraphobia may have a panic attack at any time, for no apparent reason. While the attack may last only a minute or so, the person remembers the feelings of panic so strongly that the possibility of another attack becomes terrifying. For this reason, people with agoraphobia avoid places where they might not be able to escape if a panic attack occurs. As the fear of an attack escalates, the person's world narrows.

While the specific trigger may differ, the symptoms of different phobias are remarkably similar: e.g., feelings of terror and impending doom, rapid heartbeat and breathing, sweaty palms, and other features of a panic attack. Patients may experience severe anxiety symptoms in anticipating a phobic trigger. For example, someone who is afraid to fly may begin having episodes of pounding heart and sweating palms at the mere thought of getting on a plane in two weeks.

A mental health professional can diagnose phobias after a detailed interview and discussion of both mental and physical symptoms. Social phobia is often associated with other anxiety disorders, depression, or substance abuse.

Phobias Can Be Easily Treated

People who have a specific phobia that is easy to avoid (such as snakes) and that doesn't interfere with their lives may not need to get help. When phobias do interfere with a person's daily life, a combination of psychotherapy and medication can be quite effective. While most health insurance covers some form of mental health care, most do not cover outpatient care completely, and most have a yearly or lifetime maximum.

FAST FACT

Batrachophobia is the fear of frogs.

Medication can block the feelings of panic, and when combined with cognitive-behavioral therapy, can be quite effective in reducing specific phobias and agoraphobia.

Cognitive-behavioral therapy adds a cognitive approach to more traditional behavioral therapy. It teaches patients how to change their thoughts, behavior, and attitudes, while providing techniques to lessen anxiety, such as deep breathing, muscle relaxation, and refocusing.

One cognitive-behavioral therapy is desensitization (also known as exposure therapy), in which people are gradually exposed to the frightening object or event until they become used to it and their physical symptoms decrease. For example, someone who is afraid of snakes might first be shown a photo of a snake. Once the person can look at a photo without anxiety, he might then be shown a video of a snake. Each step is repeated until the symptoms of fear (such as pounding heart and sweating palms) disappear. Eventually, the person might reach the point where he can actually touch a live snake. Three-fourths of patients are significantly improved with this type of treatment.

Another more dramatic cognitive-behavioral approach is called flooding. It exposes the person immediately to the feared object or situation. The person remains in the situation until the anxiety lessens.

Several drugs are used to treat specific phobias by controlling symptoms and helping to prevent panic attacks. These include anti-anxiety drugs (benzodiazepines) such as alprazolam (Xanax) or diazepam (Valium). Blood pressure medications called beta blockers, such as propranolol (Inderal) and atenolol (Tenormin), appear to work well in the treatment of circumscribed social phobia, when anxiety gets in the way of performance, such as public speaking. These drugs reduce overstimulation, thereby controlling the physical symptoms of anxiety.

In addition, some antidepressants may be effective when used together with cognitive-behavioral therapy.

A Cross-Section of Phobias

Phobias	Fear of...
Acrophobia	Heights
Agoraphobia	Being in an open public place
Ailurophobia	Cats
Claustrophobia	Small enclosures
Cynophobia	Dogs
Dromophobia	Crossing the street
Gerascophobia	Growing old
Hematophobia	Blood
Iatrophobia	Going to the doctor
Laliophobia	Speaking
Misophobia	Being contaminated by dirt
Musophobia	Mice
Necrophobia	Death and dead things
Ophthalmophobia	Being stared at
Phobophobia	Phobias
Toxicophobia	Poison
Triskaidekaphobia	The number thirteen
Xenophobia	Foreigners and strangers

Taken from: Compiled by the editors.

These include the monoamine oxidase inhibitors (MAO inhibitors) phenelzine (Nardil) and tranylcypromine (Parnate), as well as selective serotonin reuptake inhibitors (SSRIs) like fluoxetine (Prozac), paroxetine (Paxil), sertraline (Zoloft) and fluvoxamine (Luvox).

A medication that shows promise as a treatment for social phobia is valproic acid (Depakene or Depakote), which is usually prescribed to treat seizures or to prevent migraine headaches. Researchers conducting a twelve-week trial with 17 patients found that about half the patients experienced a significant improvement in their social anxiety symptoms while taking the medication. Further studies are underway.

In all types of phobias, symptoms may be eased by lifestyle changes, such as:

- eliminating caffeine
- cutting down on alcohol
- eating a good diet
- getting plenty of exercise
- reducing stress

Treating agoraphobia is more difficult than other phobias because there are often so many fears involved, such as open spaces, traffic, elevators, and escalators. Treatment includes cognitive-behavioral therapy with antidepressants or anti-anxiety drugs. Paxil and Zoloft are used to treat panic disorders with or without agoraphobia.

The Fine Line Between Fear and Phobia

Leah Paulos

Leah Paulos is a writer who addresses many lifestyle-related topics for teens. In this selection she examines the differences between fear and phobia and cites several examples of otherwise normal teens who have specific phobias. Paulos describes the normal emotion of fear and explains the physiological reasons why fear is a healthy emotion. She discusses the ways that normal fears become irrational phobias. Phobias affect approximately 10 percent of adolescents, the author notes.

Every time Lamont B., 16, of Brooklyn, N.Y., goes near a window inside a high building, his heart begins to pound and he starts sweating. "I'm terrified of heights," he explains. "I can't go on rooftops or terraces or near cliff edges without getting dizzy and needing to get away." Lamont suffers from a common fear that doctors call acrophobia, or fear of heights.

SOURCE: Leah Paulos, "Scared Silly: What's the Difference Between a Healthy Fear and a Phobia?" *Current Health 2*, vol. 33, October 2006, pp. 8–14. Copyright © 2006 Weekly Reader Corp. Reproduced by permission.

But don't assume that Lamont is a fearful person in general. He has plenty of friends and does well in school. Lamont regularly performs his own raps at school talent shows, the kind of activity that makes many people choke up! In fact, stage fright and the fear of speaking in public are among the most common teen phobias.

What causes a person to fear one thing and not another? And what's the difference between a true phobia and an ordinary, everyday fear?

Fear Keeps Us Safe

Fear, which helps keep us out of danger, is a complicated feeling. Need proof? People dislike fear and try their best to avoid it; yet many line up for roller coasters and horror movies. Television shows such as *Fear Factor* are also very popular. Experts say there's a fine line between fear and phobia.

Fear is a normal, and an important, human reaction to something that seems dangerous. "It kicks into effect when we feel threatened to help us either fight off the danger or run away," says Dr. David Fassler, a child and adolescent psychiatrist in Burlington, Vt. When a person is scared, he or she goes through physical changes known as the fight-or-flight reaction. Blood pressure increases and heart rate speeds up to pump blood to the large muscles used to run away. The sweat glands produce perspiration to cool the body. So if you're riding your bike and a car swerves too close to you, you can speed away more easily.

Lamont experienced that reaction recently: "One time I was walking to the video game store, and I walked by a lot [where] I didn't know there was a dog. It started barking at me, and I started running. My body started moving on its own. I was moving without knowing where it was going. I felt like I could run faster than I had ever run in my life."

Sometimes fear is triggered by a loud noise, such as the pop of a balloon or a loud clap of thunder. Often,

People dressed as zombies at a haunted house are ready to scare visitors. Many people enjoy frightening situations like this because they are in control and they know that no one will get hurt. (AP Images)

a new or unknown situation sets off our sensors for potential danger. Young people experience more fear than adults do, because they face unfamiliar events and circumstances more frequently. Many teens fear being embarrassed in front of friends or classmates, speaking in public, or being rejected. Fear can be more severe when a person feels out of control or unable to escape. That is why many people enjoy haunted houses, horror movies, and bungee jumping. They experience the physical sensations of fear, which can be thrilling, but they're in control. They know that the event will end and that no one will really get hurt!

Phobias Are Fears Out of Control

Lamont's fear of heights, which causes him to experience the body's normal fight-or-flight reaction in a situation that's not actually dangerous, is considered a phobia. "A phobia is a persistent fear of a specific object or situation that's strong and irrational," says Fassler. Lamont knows he's not going to be swept up and out the window of a building, but that knowledge doesn't keep his mind from telling his body that danger is lurking.

James A., 15, of Sherman Oaks, Calif., also suffers from a phobia: arachnophobia, or fear of spiders. "Even if I see a picture of a spider in a book, I tense up, my heart starts beating fast, and I feel like I have to get away," James says. "I know a photo of a bug can't hurt me, but I still get freaked out. I also imagine spiders in my clothes sometimes." That is another common characteristic of phobias: The sufferer spends a lot of time thinking about the fear and tries hard to avoid it.

Why do these otherwise calm, cool, and collected teens get so bent out of shape by things that are usually harmless? Phobias are often caused by something scary that happened earlier in a person's life. "When I was really little, I saw [the movie] *Arachnophobia*, and that might have been the start," James says. Experts claim that it's also common to develop a phobia after observing a parent's fear.

About one in 10 adolescents suffers from a phobia that's strong enough to affect his or her daily life. "Phobias can be treated," says Jerilyn Ross, director of the Ross Center for Anxiety and Related Disorders. "The biggest problem is that teenagers don't ask for help." If a phobia is preventing you from going to school, hanging out with friends, or doing other daily activities, it's time to seek help. Treatment often includes a combination of relaxation exercises and gradual exposure to the object of your phobia with the help of a psychiatrist or psychologist. The goal: getting your brain to gradually realize that something that seems scary actually isn't.

> **FAST FACT**
>
> Two to three times more women suffer from phobias than do men.

Doctors consider phobias a type of anxiety disorder. Anxiety refers to a feeling of nervousness, worry, or stress about something that's happening in the future. "Some anxiety in life is normal," says Ross. It can even be beneficial. If you feel anxious about a final exam, for example, you might study extra hard and ace it. But if anxiety "gets too intense or you have obsessive worries, talk to an adult," Ross says. . . .

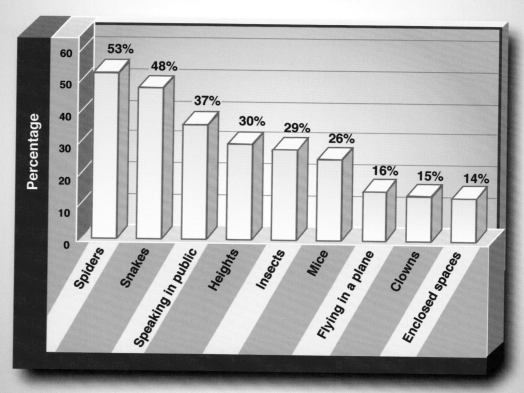

Common Teenage Fears and Phobias

Percentage of 9th- through 12th-grade students who are "very afraid" of:

Percentage

- Spiders: 53%
- Snakes: 48%
- Speaking in public: 37%
- Heights: 30%
- Insects: 29%
- Mice: 26%
- Flying in a plane: 16%
- Clowns: 15%
- Enclosed spaces: 14%

Taken from: Leah Paulos, "Scared Silly," *Current Health 2*, October 2006.

Famous People Have Phobias, Too

Many celebrities suffer from phobias. Here's a sampling.

Johnny Depp and Sean "Diddy" Combs are freaked out by clowns. They have clourophobia. . . .

Soccer star David Beckham is ataxophobic, a person who fears disorder. Pssst! We hear he makes sure that each shirt in his closet is hung according to color and that each can of soda in the fridge is perfectly lined up.

Tyra Banks has a fear of dolphins but agreed to conquer her fear by swimming with them for her TV talk show.

The Treatments Available for Phobias and Anxiety Are Varied

National Institute of Mental Health

This article is a taken from a health publication distributed by the National Institute of Mental Health, a division of the U.S. government's National Institutes of Health. It discusses different methods of treating different anxiety disorders, including medication and types of psychotherapy such as cognitive-behavioral therapy (CBT). In addition to traditional treatment, meditation, exercise, and other forms of stress management are also encouraged.

In general, anxiety disorders are treated with medication, specific types of psychotherapy, or both. Treatment choices depend on the problem and the person's preference. Before treatment begins, a doctor must conduct a careful diagnostic evaluation to determine whether a person's symptoms are caused by an anxiety disorder or a physical problem. If an anxiety disorder is diagnosed,

SOURCE: National Institute of Mental Health, "Anxiety Disorders," online publication, National Institutes of Health, 2008.

the type of disorder or the combination of disorders that are present must be identified, as well as any coexisting conditions, such as depression or substance abuse. Sometimes alcoholism, depression, or other coexisting conditions have such a strong effect on the individual that treating the anxiety disorder must wait until the coexisting conditions are brought under control.

People with anxiety disorders who have already received treatment should tell their current doctor about that treatment in detail. If they received medication, they should tell their doctor what medication was used, what the dosage was at the beginning of treatment, whether the dosage was increased or decreased while they were under treatment, what side effects occurred, and whether the treatment helped them become less anxious. If they received psychotherapy, they should describe the type of therapy, how often they attended sessions, and whether the therapy was useful.

Often people believe that they have "failed" at treatment or that the treatment didn't work for them when, in fact, it was not given for an adequate length of time or was administered incorrectly. Sometimes people must try several different treatments or combinations of treatment before they find the one that works for them.

Medications

Medication will not cure anxiety disorders, but it can keep them under control while the person receives psychotherapy. Medication must be prescribed by physicians, usually psychiatrists, who can either offer psychotherapy themselves or work as a team with psychologists, social workers, or counselors who provide psychotherapy. The principal medications used for anxiety disorders are antidepressants, anti-anxiety drugs, and beta-blockers to control some of the physical symptoms. With proper treatment, many people with anxiety disorders can lead normal, fulfilling lives.

Antidepressants

Antidepressants were developed to treat depression but are also effective for anxiety disorders. Although these medications begin to alter brain chemistry after the very first dose, their full effect requires a series of changes to occur; it is usually about 4 to 6 weeks before symptoms start to fade. It is important to continue taking these medications long enough to let them work.

SSRIs

Some of the newest antidepressants are called selective serotonin reuptake inhibitors, or SSRIs. SSRIs alter the

There are a number of treatments available for phobias and anxiety disorders, including several medications. (© 2008 /Jupiterimages)

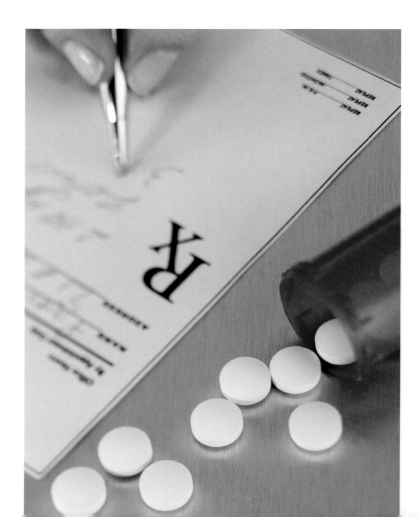

How SSRIs Work

When neurotransmitters such as serotonin bind with receptors on a neighboring neuron, they carry the impulse to the next cell. But in someone with symptoms of depression, the cell that released the serotonin may reabsorb it too quickly. As a result, there may not be enough serotonin available to bind to the next cell and allow the signal to pass. SSRIs slow the reuptake of serotonin, leaving more of this neurotransmitter in the synapse. This permits it to work for a longer time, improving the transmission of nerve impulses.

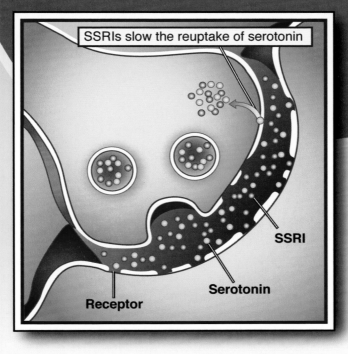

SSRIs slow the reuptake of serotonin

SSRI

Serotonin

Receptor

Taken from: Michael J. Mufson, "Coping with Anxieties and Phobias," *Harvard Special Health Report*, July 2006.

levels of the neurotransmitter serotonin in the brain, which, like other neurotransmitters, helps brain cells communicate with one another.

Fluoxetine (Prozac®), sertraline (Zoloft®), escitalopram (Lexapro®), paroxetine (Paxil®), and citalopram (Celexa®) are some of the SSRIs commonly prescribed for panic disorder, OCD [obsessive-compulsive disorder], PTSD [post-traumatic stress disorder], and social phobia.

FAST FACT

Untreated phobias lead to other problems such as depression, alcoholism, and low self-esteem.

SSRIs are also used to treat panic disorder when it occurs in combination with OCD, social phobia, or depression. Venlafaxine (Effexor®), a drug closely related to the SSRIs, is used to treat GAD [generalized anxiety disorder]. These medications are started at low doses and gradually increased until they have a beneficial effect.

SSRIs have fewer side effects than older antidepressants, but they sometimes produce slight nausea or jitters when people first start to take them. These symptoms fade with time. Some people also experience sexual dysfunction with SSRIs, which may be helped by adjusting the dosage or switching to another SSRI.

Tricyclics

Tricyclics are older than SSRIs and work as well as SSRIs for anxiety disorders other than OCD. They are also started at low doses that are gradually increased. They sometimes cause dizziness, drowsiness, dry mouth, and weight gain, which can usually be corrected by changing the dosage or switching to another tricyclic medication.

Tricyclics include imipramine (Tofranil®), which is prescribed for panic disorder and GAD, and clomiramine (Anafranil®), which is the only tricyclic antidepressant useful for treating OCD.

MAOIs

Monoamine oxidase inhibitors (MAOIs) are the oldest class of antidepressant medications. The MAOIs most commonly prescribed for anxiety disorders are phenelzine (Nardil®), followed by tranylcypromine (Parnate®), and isocarboxazid (Marplan®), which are useful in treating panic disorder and social phobia. People who take MAOIs cannot eat a variety of foods and beverages (including cheese and red wine) that contain tyramine or take certain medications, including some types of birth control pills, pain relievers (such as Advil®, Motrin®, or Tylenol®), cold and allergy medications, and herbal supplements; these substances can interact with MAOIs to cause dangerous increases in blood pressure. The development of a new MAOI skin patch may help lessen these risks. MAOIs can also react with SSRIs to produce a serious condition called "serotonin syndrome," which can cause confusion, hallucinations, increased sweating, muscle stiffness, seizures, changes in blood pressure or heart rhythm, and other potentially life-threatening conditions.

Anti-Anxiety Drugs

High-potency benzodiazepines combat anxiety and have few side effects other than drowsiness. Because people can get used to them and may need higher and higher doses to get the same effect, benzodiazepines are generally prescribed for short periods of time, especially for people who have abused drugs or alcohol and who become dependent on medication easily. One exception to this rule is people with panic disorder, who can take benzodiazepines for up to a year without harm.

Clonazepam (Klonopin®) is used for social phobia and GAD, lorazepam (Ativan®) is helpful for panic disorder, and alprazolam (Xanax®) is useful for both panic disorder and GAD.

Some people experience withdrawal symptoms if they stop taking benzodiazepines abruptly instead of tapering off, and anxiety can return once the medication is stopped. These potential problems have led some physicians to shy away from using these drugs or to use them in inadequate doses.

Buspirone (Buspar®), an azapirone, is a newer anti-anxiety medication used to treat GAD. Possible side effects include dizziness, headaches, and nausea. Unlike benzodiazepines, buspirone must be taken consistently for at least 2 weeks to achieve an anti-anxiety effect.

Beta-Blockers

Beta-blockers, such as propranolol (Inderal®), which is used to treat heart conditions, can prevent the physical symptoms that accompany certain anxiety disorders, particularly social phobia. When a feared situation can be predicted (such as giving a speech), a doctor may prescribe a beta-blocker to keep physical symptoms of anxiety under control.

Psychotherapy

Psychotherapy involves talking with a trained mental health professional, such as a psychiatrist, psychologist, social worker, or counselor, to discover what caused an anxiety disorder and how to deal with its symptoms.

Cognitive-Behavioral Therapy

Cognitive-Behavioral Therapy (CBT) is very useful in treating anxiety disorders. The cognitive part helps people change the thinking patterns that support their fears, and the behavioral part helps people change the way they react to anxiety-provoking situations.

For example, CBT can help people with panic disorder learn that their panic attacks are not really heart attacks and help people with social phobia learn how to overcome the belief that others are always watching and judging them. When people are ready to confront their fears, they are shown how to use exposure techniques to desensitize themselves to situations that trigger their anxieties.

People with OCD who fear dirt and germs are encouraged to get their hands dirty and wait increasing amounts of time before washing them. The therapist helps the person cope with the anxiety that waiting produces; after the exercise has been repeated a number of times, the anxiety diminishes. People with social phobia may be encouraged to spend time in feared social situations without giving in to the temptation to flee and to make small social blunders and observe how people respond to them. Since the response is usually far less harsh than the person fears, these anxieties are lessened. People with PTSD may be supported through recalling their traumatic event in a safe situation, which helps reduce the fear it produces. CBT therapists also teach deep breathing and other types of exercises to relieve anxiety and encourage relaxation.

Exposure-based behavioral therapy has been used for many years to treat specific phobias. The person gradually encounters the object or situation that is feared, perhaps at first only through pictures or tapes, then later face-to-face.

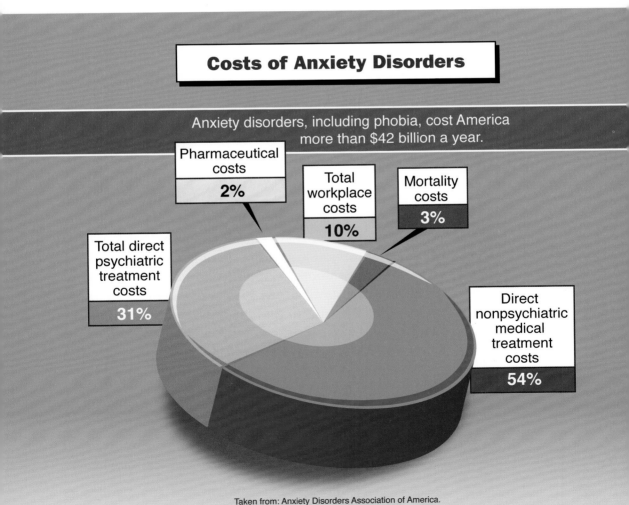

Costs of Anxiety Disorders

Anxiety disorders, including phobia, cost America more than $42 billion a year.

Pharmaceutical costs
2%

Total workplace costs
10%

Mortality costs
3%

Total direct psychiatric treatment costs
31%

Direct nonpsychiatric medical treatment costs
54%

Taken from: Anxiety Disorders Association of America.

Often the therapist will accompany the person to a feared situation to provide support and guidance.

CBT is undertaken when people decide they are ready for it and with their permission and cooperation. To be effective, the therapy must be directed at the person's specific anxieties and must be tailored to his or her needs. There are no side effects other than the discomfort of temporarily increased anxiety.

CBT or behavioral therapy often lasts about 12 weeks. It may be conducted individually or with a group of people who have similar problems. Group therapy is particularly effective for social phobia. Often "homework" is assigned for participants to complete between sessions. There is some evidence that the benefits of CBT last longer than those of medication for people with panic disorder, and the same may be true for OCD, PTSD, and social phobia. If a disorder recurs at a later date, the same therapy can be used to treat it successfully a second time.

Medication can be combined with psychotherapy for specific anxiety disorders, and this is the best treatment approach for many people. . . .

Ways to Make Treatment More Effective

Many people with anxiety disorders benefit from joining a self-help or support group and sharing their problems and achievements with others. Internet chat rooms can also be useful in this regard, but any advice received over the Internet should be used with caution, as Internet acquaintances have usually never seen each other and false identities are common. Talking with a trusted friend or member of the clergy can also provide support, but it is not a substitute for care from a mental health professional.

Stress management techniques and meditation can help people with anxiety disorders calm themselves and may enhance the effects of therapy. There is preliminary evidence that aerobic exercise may have a calming effect.

Since caffeine, certain illicit drugs, and even some over-the-counter cold medications can aggravate the symptoms of anxiety disorders, they should be avoided. . . .

The family is very important in the recovery of a person with an anxiety disorder. Ideally, the family should be supportive but not help perpetuate their loved one's symptoms. Family members should not trivialize the disorder or demand improvement without treatment.

Specific Phobias, Social Phobias, and Agoraphobias Respond Well to Treatment

Lynne L. Hall

Lynne L. Hall is a writer from Birmingham, Alabama. In this article she examines the origin of various phobias and their treatment. She categorizes phobias into three groups: simple phobias, social phobias, and agoraphobia. Noting that doctors are not completely certain why phobias arise, the author asserts that many can be treated by systematically desensitizing the patient in a step-by-step process. Social phobias and agoraphobia are more complex and may be caused by physiological problems. Treatments, Hall says, may include behavioral therapy and a variety of medications.

From 50 yards away, you see the animal approaching. Silently it watches you as it slinks ever so much closer with each padded step. Stay calm, you tell yourself. There's nothing to fear.

But suddenly, panic seizes you in a death grip, squeezing the breath out of you and turning your knees to Jell-O. Your heart starts slam-dancing inside your chest, your

SOURCE: Lynne L. Hall, "Fighting Phobias: The Things That Go Bump in the Night," U.S. Food and Drug Administration.

mouth turns to cotton, and your palms are so sweaty you'd swear they'd sprung a leak. You'd escape this terrifying confrontation, if only you could make your legs work!

Just what is this wild and dangerous animal making you hyperventilate and turning your legs to rubber? A man-eating tiger, hungry for a meal? A lioness bent on protecting her cubs? Guess again. That's Tabby, your neighbor's ordinary house cat, sauntering your way. Ridiculous, right? How can anyone experience so much fear at the sight of such an innocuous animal? If you're one of the thousands who suffer from galeophobia—the fear of cats—or any one of hundreds of other phobias, sheer panic at the appearance of everyday objects, situations or feelings is a regular occurrence.

Irrational Fears Affect Many People

A phobia is an intense, unrealistic fear of an object, an event, or a feeling. An estimated 18 percent of the U.S. adult population suffers from some kind of phobia, and a person can develop a phobia of anything—elevators, clocks, mushrooms, closed spaces, open spaces. Exposure to these trigger the rapid breathing, pounding heartbeat, and sweaty palms of panic.

There are three defined types of phobias:

- specific or simple phobias—fear of an object or situation, such as spiders, heights or flying
- social phobias—fear of embarrassment or humiliation in social settings
- agoraphobia—fear of being away from a safe place.

No one knows for sure how phobias develop. Often, there is no explanation for the fear. In many cases, though, a person can readily identify an event or trauma—such as being chased by a dog—that triggered the phobia. What puzzles experts is why some people who experience such

Specific phobias are fears of distinct situations or objects, such as black cats. (© 2008/Jupiterimages)

an event develop a phobia and others do not. Many psychologists believe the cause lies in a combination of genetic predisposition mixed with environmental and social causes.

Phobic disorders are classified as part of the group of anxiety disorders, which includes panic disorder, post-traumatic stress disorder, and obsessive-compulsive disorder. Several drugs regulated by the Food and Drug Administration are now being used to treat phobias and other anxiety disorders.

Most Phobias Are Specific

A person can develop a specific phobia of anything, but in most cases the phobia is shared by many and has a name. Animal phobias—cynophobia (dogs), equino-phobia (horses), zoophobia (all animals)—are common. So are arachnophobia (spiders) and ophidiophobia (snakes). And, of course, there's the fear of flying (pterygophobia), heights (acrophobia), and confined spaces (claustrophobia).

"One of the most common phobias is the fear of dentists [odontiatophobia]," says Sheryl Jackson, Ph.D., a clinical psychologist and associate professor at the University of Alabama at Birmingham. "People who suffer with this phobia will literally let their teeth rot out because they are afraid to go to a dentist."

Jackson says that most specific phobias do not cause a serious disruption in a person's life, and, consequently, sufferers do not seek professional help. Instead, they find ways to avoid whatever it is that triggers their panic, or they simply endure the distress felt when they encounter it. Some may also consult their physicians, requesting medication to help them through a situation, such as an unavoidable plane trip for someone who is phobic about flying.

Drugs prescribed for these short-term situations include benzodiazepine anti-anxiety agents. These medications include two approved for treating anxiety disorders: Xanax (alprazolam) and Valium (diazepam). Beta blockers such as Inderal (propranolol) and Tenormin (atenolol), approved for controlling high blood pressure and some heart problems, have been acknowledged, partly on the basis of controlled trials, to be helpful in certain situations in which anxiety interferes with performance, such as public speaking.

Some phobias cause significant problems that require long-term professional help. "People usually seek treatment when their phobia interferes in their lives—the person who turns down promotions because he knows public speaking will be required, someone who must travel frequently but who is afraid of flying, or a woman who wants

FAST FACT

Phobias are a subset of anxiety disorders.

to have children but who has a fear of pain or blood. These are the people who seek long-term treatment," says Jackson.

While anti-anxiety medication sometimes may be used initially, systematic desensitization may also be an effective initial approach. Jackson explains that this non-drug treatment works on the theory that the more a person is exposed to the object of his phobia, the less fear that object generates.

First, the patient and therapist establish a hierarchy of feared situations, from the least to the most feared. For someone who fears elevators, for example, stepping onto the elevator causes a certain level of anxiety; going up one flight causes another level of anxiety. With each additional flight the anxiety increases until it becomes intolerable.

Therapy begins with the patient and therapist practicing the least fearful event, riding out the anxiety until the physiological symptoms subside. This step is repeated until the anxiety level is acceptable. Then the person progresses to the next step in the hierarchy. Each successive step is repeated until the physical reactions and anxious mood decrease to the point where the person can step onto an elevator and ride to the top floor without panicking.

Social Phobia Blocks Normal Social Interaction

Social phobia is a complex disorder, characterized by the fear of being criticized or humiliated in social situations. There are two types of social phobias: circumscribed, which relates to a specific situation such as "stage fright," and generalized social phobia, which involves fear of a variety of social situations.

People suffering from social phobia fear the scrutiny of others. They tend to be highly sensitive to criticism, and often interpret the actions of others in social gatherings as an attempt to humiliate them. They are afraid to enter into conversations for fear of saying something foolish, and may agonize for hours or days later over things they did say.

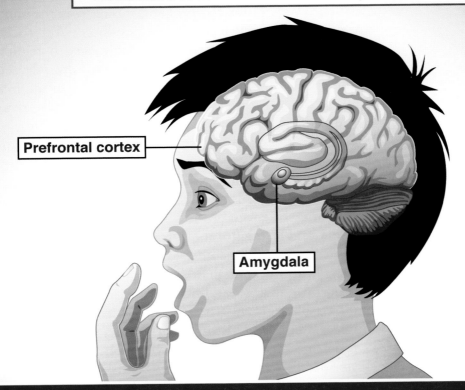

How the Brain Controls Fear

The amygdala and the prefrontal cortex are two areas of the brain identified as playing key roles in the fear control process. This knowledge is helpful to researchers of new medicines to treat phobias.

Prefrontal cortex

Amygdala

Taken from: Society for Neuroscience.

"I always believed that everybody else knew the secret to enjoying themselves in social situations, that I was the only one who was so afraid," says Lorraine from Birmingham, Ala., who asked that her last name not be used. "For a long time, I avoided as many situations as possible, even talking on the telephone. After a while, the loneliness and boredom would overwhelm me, and I would try again. I wanted to have fun, but I never really enjoyed myself because of the anxiety I felt. I always believed that others were looking at me and judging me."

Many people with social phobia are so sensitive to the scrutiny of others that they avoid eating or drinking in public, using public restrooms, or signing a check in the presence of another. Social phobia may often be associated with depression or alcohol abuse.

Neurotransmitter-receptor abnormalities in the brain are suspected to play a part in the development of social phobias. Neurotransmitters are substances such as norepinephrine, dopamine and serotonin that are released in the brain. The substance then either excites or inhibits a target ceil. Disorders in the physiology of these neurotransmitters are thought to be the cause of a variety of psychiatric illnesses.

Negative social experiences, such as being rejected by peers or suffering some type of embarrassment in public, and poor social skills also seem to be factors, and social phobia may be related to low self-esteem, lack of assertiveness, and feelings of inferiority.

Treatment can include cognitive-behavior therapy and medications, though no drug is approved specifically for social phobia. In addition to the anti-anxiety drugs and beta-blockers, medications may include the monoamine oxidase (MAO) inhibitor antidepressants Nardil (phenelzine) and Parnate (tranylcypromine), and serotonin specific reuptake inhibitors (SSRIs) such as Prozac (fluoxetine), Paxil (paroxetine), Zoloft (sertraline), and Luvox (fluvoxamine). Of the latter four drugs, Prozac,

Zoloft and Paxil are approved for depression; Prozac, Paxil, Luvox, and Zoloft are approved for obsessive-compulsive disorder; and Paxil is approved for panic disorder.

Chris Sletten, Ph.D., a clinical psychologist and behavioral medicine specialist at the Mayo Clinic, says the use of SSRIs with behavior therapy is becoming more popular in the treatment of social phobia. Because there are fewer side effects associated with these drugs and a very low addiction potential, practitioners are more comfortable prescribing them. Plus, the antidepressant action of these drugs is helpful in treating patients who suffer from depression in addition to social phobia, he says.

"My therapist prescribed Prozac, and it has been an absolute godsend for me," Lorraine says. "After only a couple of months taking it, those voices in my head, the ones that always assured me that everyone was judging me—and finding me lacking—just seemed to shut up. I didn't feel high or drugged in any way. I felt like I always thought a normal person would feel. It's not a complete cure, of course. I still feel anxiety in social situations. But I don't avoid them as much. In fact, I actually pick up the phone now and ask friends to dinner, and I can relax enough to have fun. It's a whole new life for me."

Agoraphobia Causes Unexplained Panic Attacks

Agoraphobia comes from Greek, meaning literally "fear of the marketplace," but it usually is defined as a fear of open spaces. Sletten says it stems more from the fear of being someplace where you will not be able to escape. It is closely identified with panic disorder, and in many cases, agoraphobia is directly related to the fear of experiencing a panic attack in public.

A person with panic disorder suffers sudden bouts of panic for no apparent reason. These attacks can occur anywhere at any time. One minute everything is fine, the next the person is engulfed by a feeling of terror. The heart races, breathing comes in gasps, and the entire body trembles. The attack may last only minutes, but its memory is etched indelibly in the brain, and the anticipation of another causes almost as much terror as the attack itself.

People who suffer agoraphobia avoid places and situations where they feel escape would be difficult in case an attack occurs. This could be anywhere—the grocery store, a shopping mail, the office. As the fear of an attack increases, the agoraphobic's world narrows to only a few places where he or she feels safe. In the most severe cases, this is limited to the home.

Agoraphobia is the most disabling of all the phobias, and treatment is difficult because there are so many associated fears—the fear of crowds, of elevators, of traffic. As with social phobias, treatment involves behavioral therapy combined with anti-anxiety or antidepressant medications, or both. Paxil has received FDA approval for use in treating panic disorders with or without agoraphobia, and at press time, Zoloft was being considered for this additional use.

"The most important thing for people with phobias to remember," says Sletten, "is that phobic disorders do respond well to treatment. It's not something they have to continue to suffer with."

Phobias Can Start at a Young Age

Lidia Wasowicz

This article from UPI examines the increasing incidence of psychiatric conditions appearing in children of younger and younger ages. The author, Lidia Wasowicz, notes that while 13 in 100 children and adolescents have anxiety disorders, and about half of those experience secondary problems such as social phobias and depression, most are not getting diagnosed. In 2002 President George W. Bush created the New Freedom Commission on Mental Health to study and make recommendations for this growing concern. Detractors worry, however, that the screening programs suggested by the commission are too intrusive into peoples' private lives. Skeptics also argue that the lines are being blurred between mental illness and normal everyday struggles. Still, many schools and community-based children's programs agree the prevalence of anxiety and depression in children and the resultant behavioral problems is becoming more apparent.

Long thought to fly above children's air space, psychiatric conditions such as depression have only in recent years started appearing on the pediatric radar.

SOURCE: Lidia Wasowicz, "PedMed: Too Many Troubled Kids," *UPI online*, January 25, 2006. Reproduced by permission.

Anxiety disorders are now estimated to affect 13 in 100 children and adolescents ages 9 to 17, about half of whom also experience a second mental or behavioral ailment, such as social phobias, obsessive-compulsive disorder or depression.

Others may suffer a co-existing physical malady that commands—and confounds—treatment, according to a report by the Substance Abuse and Mental Health Services Administration.

"[Attention-deficit/hyperactivity disorder] is the most commonly treated diagnosis, but in terms of prevalence, many, many more children have anxiety disorders, but they're not hitting the radar because they're not getting identified by way of school," notes clinical psychologist Tamar Chansky. He is director of the Children's Center for OCD and Anxiety in Plymouth Meeting, Pa., and author of "Freeing Your Child from Anxiety" (Broadway Books, 2004) and "Freeing Your Child from Obsessive-Compulsive Disorder" (Crown Publishers, 2000).

> **FAST FACT**
>
> Social phobias are chronic and do not go away without treatment.

Ensuring they're brought into focus is one of the goals of the president's New Freedom Commission on Mental Health, created by George W. Bush in 2002 to study and recommend ways to beef up the service-delivery system.

The group has its detractors who fear the coming of an era of mental McCarthyism with the setup of screening programs the commission has recommended for detecting behavioral and emotional disturbances in children and teens. The group's proponents see it as a long-overdue, much-needed compass for pointing out the directions for reform.

"Early childhood is a critical period for the onset of emotional and behavioral impairments," the commission reported in July 2003. "Each year, young children are expelled from preschools and childcare facilities for severely disruptive behaviors and emotional disorders."

Two years later, a survey by the Yale Child Study Center of 3,898 state-funded preschools serving some 800,000 tots in 40 states found nearly seven in 1,000 face the ultimate sanction for misbehaving. That's three times the rate at which their older counterparts are tossed out of elementary, middle and high schools.

Stressful and embarrassing events in childhood can lead to social phobia. (© **John Birdsall/The Image Works**)

The analysis showed boys are 4.6 times more likely than girls to be asked to leave, and black youngsters have a dismissal rate 1.7 times that of whites, 2.3 times that of Hispanics and 5.5 times that of Asians.

In the study of public, Head Start, non- and for-profit, faith-based and other community programs, New Mexico topped the list, with 21 preschoolers per 1,000 shown the door, while Kentucky reported no forced exits in this age group.

"Since children develop rapidly, delivering mental health services and supports early and swiftly is necessary to avoid permanent consequences," the president's commission recommends.

The system has failed in both regards, contends a far-reaching, and to critics far-flung, survey of 9,282 Americans over 17, which traced the roots of most mental illnesses to untreated childhood problems.

The massive $20 million, once-a-decade assessment, presented as a series of papers published in the Archives of General Psychiatry, found a mind-numbing 46 percent of those questioned had suffered a mental illness at some point in life. Half of them showed the first signs of abnormality by age 14, the authors said.

The survey, funded by the government, health research foundations and pharmaceutical companies, posed questions about sustained sadness, alcohol abuse, fretful fears or other symptoms that might meet the criteria for a disorder, as described in the American Psychiatric Association's Diagnostic and Statistical Manual of Mental Disorders. The DSM is the reference guide used by professionals to classify psychiatric symptoms.

Skeptics seized upon the startling statistics to support their long-standing contention that by continually broadening the defining features, psychiatrists are blunting the distinction between wellness and illness and giving everyday struggles a sickly spin.

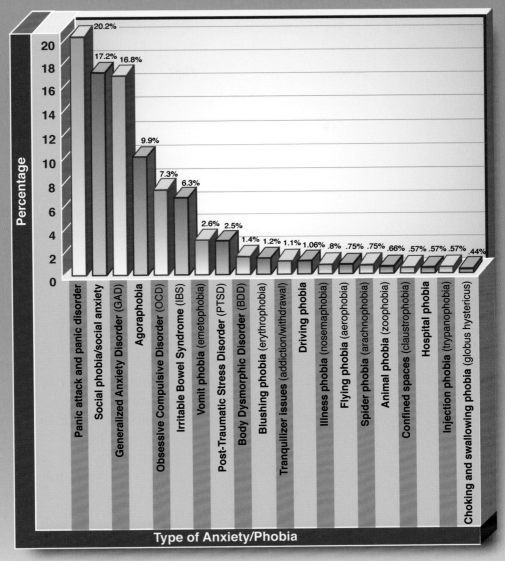

Phobia Prevalence in the United Kingdom

Taken from: National Phobics' Society Survey, 2005–2006. www.phobics-society.org.uk.

Dr. Thomas Insel, director of the National Institute of Mental Health, however, insisted the report rightly reinforced the notion of mental maladies as "the chronic diseases of the young" that need to be identified and nipped in the bud before ripening into full-blown illness.

As if echoing that sentiment, counselors in 68 percent of high schools, 57 percent of middle schools and 55 percent of primary schools deemed student depression a "moderate" or "great" problem—more serious than violence, including bullying, fighting and use of weapons.

Anxiety got equal billing on the list of concerns at more than 40 percent of campuses at all three educational levels. The survey of more than 1,400 mental-health professionals was conducted in 2004 by the Annenberg Public Policy Center at the University of Pennsylvania.

Results of a study commissioned by the National Alliance for the Mentally Ill and Abbott Laboratories suggest college proves no panacea. In the study, half of students judged their mental health to be below average or poor, one in three reported periods of prolonged depression, one in four entertained suicidal thoughts and one in seven found it difficult to function because of psychiatric problems.

These include bipolar disorder, a condition that shoves its targets onto a mood-jolting rollercoaster ride between manic highs of sleep-shunning euphoria and grandiose delusions and depressive lows of strength-sapping despair and sense of worthlessness.

Psychiatrists suspect the disorder—until recently rarely diagnosed in youth—may in fact affect up to one-third of the 3.4 million depressed children and adolescents in the United States, reports the National Mental Health Association, a non-profit advocacy group that is partially supported by pharmaceutical companies.

CHAPTER 2

The Many Treatments of Phobias

Hypnosis Alleviates Phobia-Induced Anxiety

Robert Hill and Glynn Bannon-Ryder

In the following article Robert Hill, who is with the Addictions Directorate in South London, and Glynn Bannon-Ryder, who is with the Maudsley National Health System Trust in London, discuss the use of hypnosis in treating patients with phobias. They describe the treatment of a thirty-seven-year-old patient who had developed driving phobia after experiencing a number of traffic accidents. They explain that her phobia was interfering with both her professional life as a community psychiatric nurse as well as her personal life. The authors describe how four sessions of hypnosis were sufficient to help the patient reduce her fears enough for her to make a long-distance trip that she had been avoiding for years. In a one-year follow-up they note that the patient was continuing to make progress.

Photo on previous page. There are many treatments available for phobias. The first step is to talk to your doctor. **(Siri Stafford/ Riser/Getty Images)**

The client was a 37-year-old woman who worked as a community psychiatric nurse in a busy London hospital. She passed her driving test on the fifth

SOURCE: Robert Hill and Glynn Bannon-Ryder, "The Use of Hypnosis in the Treatment of Driving Phobia," *Contemporary Hypnosis*, vol. 22, 2005, pp. 99–103. Copyright © 2005 by John Wiley and Sons, Ltd. This material is used by permission.

occasion aged 18. Almost immediately afterwards, she was involved in four rather dramatic, but not seriously injurious, accidents. Three of these occurred when she was a passenger and two while she was driving. Her first accident, however, occurred when she was a young girl travelling with her parents. Here the car was involved in a six-car pile up. There were no serious injuries, although she did recall standing in the central reservation and being very shaken. The second accident happened not long after she had passed her test. She lost control of the car after being run off the road by a drunk driver and skidded off the road, with the car teetering on the edge of a river. The third accident occurred when she was in her mid twenties and lost control of her car while approaching a roundabout. She lost her licence on this occasion and sustained some minor injuries. In the first accident as a passenger, the driver lost control on a bend and drove through a wall, with the car coming to a standstill upside down. The final major accident occurred during an overtaking manoeuvre. The car in this instance ended up rolling over onto a hedge.

None of the accidents, although potentially fatal, required hospitalization and apart from minor scarring, no serious injuries were sustained. She reported that as a result of these accidents, which happened in her early twenties, she did not travel by car for a few years. When she married, her husband drove and she was able to avoid driving until the time she retrained as a psychiatric nurse in her late twenties. When she resumed driving she would drive on familiar routes only. She was currently driving to her place of work, using one well-known route. She reported both anticipatory anxiety and anxiety while driving, saying that much of her fear derived from a lack of confidence and a propensity to assume that negative judgements were being made by others. These assumptions may have contributed to the fact that she was also very self critical of her own driving. She was aware that she was engaged in avoidance behaviour. The client was highly motivated to do something about this avoidance behaviour and wanted to be able to drive along a busy London road to her mother-in-law's as well as driving to visit her parents in the country.

The client was born in the UK, widowed with two small children and currently worked in the health service. She did not have any current medical conditions that would affect her driving and described herself as both very self critical and analytical which could sometimes have an effect upon her levels of self-confidence. She regularly employed cognitive behavioural techniques in her work with mental health clients.

Details of Assessment

Three areas were focused on in the initial assessment: 1) previous treatment; 2) knowledge and concerns about hypnosis; and 3) suggestibility, trance, and imagery favoured. A sheet devised by the author was used to assess these areas. The primary goal was to be able to travel by car to places that she was currently avoiding with three particular situations in mind: visiting her mother-in-law who lived locally; visiting her parents who lived in the countryside; and driving when going on summer holiday. In order to achieve these goals it was considered desirable to focus on a reduction in her anticipatory anxiety using hypnosis and to support her in undertaking travel related targets outside the hypnotic session. She had received no previous treatment for her driving difficulties.

The client had used hypnosis for weight control purposes previously, but with no positive effect, therefore, although sceptical, she had a good understanding of hypnotic principles and had no particular concerns about its therapeutic use. In order for her partner or family to understand the treatment she was receiving she was given a copy of a paper on the truth and type of hypnosis published in *Scientific American*. Hypnotic sessions were booked in on a two weekly basis during her lunch break.

The Creative Imagination Scale was used to assess hypnotic susceptibility and, while there are difficulties in measuring hypnosis in this way, the scale is regarded as a suitable way of introducing hypnosis to a client. She scored 29 on this scale and appeared to have good imaginal skills. In terms of favoured imagery for a relaxing or safe place she chose a tropical beach on her own.

During discussions with the author's supervisor concerning the treatment of cases of driving phobia it was

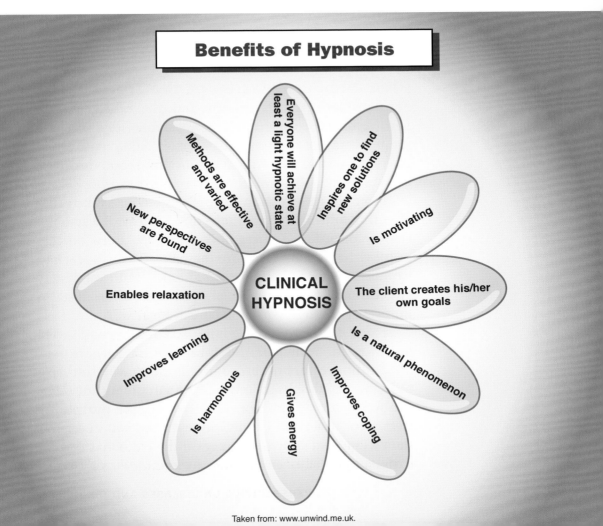

Benefits of Hypnosis

CLINICAL HYPNOSIS

Everyone will achieve at least a light hypnotic state

Methods are effective and varied

New perspectives are found

Inspires one to find new solutions

Is motivating

Enables relaxation

The client creates his/her own goals

Improves learning

Is harmonious

Gives energy

Improves coping

Is a natural phenomenon

Taken from: www.unwind.me.uk.

suggested that one means of assessing driving difficulties was to ask clients to imagine themselves driving a well-known journey and to recount this to the therapist as they are doing it. The supervisor's experience was that the more precise, detailed and slow such a description was the more indicative it was of a driving difficulty. She described her trip to work in great detail quite slowly. Theoretically it can be assumed that drivers undertake well-known journeys on an almost automatic basis. The fact that she was describing what should have been a learnt habitual act in a very slow and detailed fashion was suggestive of some attentional biases. However, given her description of herself as extremely analytic, this may reflect a facet of her personality rather than anything related to her driving difficulties.

Plan and Formulation of the Treatment

Four primary psychiatric disorders [have been identified] resulting from road traffic accidents (RTAs). These are post-traumatic stress disorder (PTSD), acute stress disorder (ASD), major depression/other mood disorders and driving phobias/other anxiety disorders.

From the information given it seemed most likely that after difficulties fitted best into the category of a phobic/anxiety disorder. [Others have] reported some success using virtual reality exposure therapy with a 35-year-old woman in which there was a reduction both in anxiety and avoidant behaviour, which were maintained at seven months. PTSD is a common consequence of traffic accidents and can be related both to their number and severity. Avoidant behaviour and/or safety behaviour are usually a prime feature of this condition along with intrusive thoughts and flashbacks related to the traumatic incident. She was not suffering from PTSD, due in all probability to the fact that none of the accidents resulted in serious injury. She did however engage in safety behaviour by travelling on familiar routes only and avoidant behaviour by avoiding certain trips altogether. Avoidance of motorways, bridges and tunnels has been found to be a common form of avoidance among clients with driving phobia. Given that she was able to undertake certain car journeys and that there was no indication that she was a particularly reckless driver, it was not necessary for her to work with a driving instructor

The client was a young woman who as the result of a number of accidents developed a pattern of avoidant behaviour in relation to travelling by car. She would only travel on certain journeys if she knew them well and would always take the same route. She was concerned about what others thought of her driving, possibly arising from the fact that the accidents in which she had been involved—landing upside down, going though a wall, overturning on a hedge, teetering on the brink of a river and driving through a roundabout—were ones in which she became a visible and powerless object subject to the curiosity of other motorists and the attention of the emergency services. She had thus developed a form of self-consciousness in relation to her driving and had also internalized the criticisms that she thought others were making of her. The fact that she lost her license on one occasion may have done much to increase this sense of being negatively judged. Thus, it was hypothesized that she did not view accidents as bringing about physical harm but social harm through looking 'foolish'. In this instance therefore the driving phobia was sustained more by the mechanisms of self-doubt and low self-esteem, prevalent in social anxiety disorders, than by fragmented and intrusive mechanisms found in PTSD arising from car accidents. One of the things that currently sustained the avoidance behaviour was the behaviour of her relatives who would do everything they could to help her to arrive at her destination without having to drive.

FAST FACT

According to one survey, hypnotherapy is effective with a 93 percent recovery rate after six sessions.

Thus they would sometimes drive to London to pick her up, or arrange to meet her at the local train station.

The treatment was designed to focus first on anticipatory anxiety and secondly on positive outcomes using hypnosis. In addition, and prior to undertaking the goals that she had set herself, the therapy aimed to get her travelling on journeys that she currently undertook using a different route.

Treatment Sessions

The first treatment session began by discussing the format it would take. We decided to discuss goals that could be completed prior to the next session before undertaking the hypnosis in order that these could be incorporated into the hypnotic procedure. The client therefore suggested that she travel to work by a different route.

The hypnotic procedure was undertaken using [standard hypnosis techniques of] a Spiegel eye roll, followed by deepening and then safe place. She was then asked to picture herself successfully completing this journey. In addition material was inserted into the hypnotic session that emphasized the fact that there were no expectations or critical judgements being made about her driving. She reported significant time distortion at the end of the session (estimating 20 minutes instead of 50).

[The second treatment session] occurred two weeks later and began by reviewing progress. She reported that an alternative trip to work had been successfully made, although it had been very busy. She also reported that she had on the spur of the moment made a trip to IKEA, which involved some very busy roads. Although she reported getting lost this was not reported as a problem, which surprised her. The goal she set before the next session was to travel to see one of her clients at home, which she had been avoiding, and to try travelling to her mother-in-law. The hypnotic session itself followed the same format as session 1.

She reported difficulties in using self-hypnosis because she became easily distracted and asked whether it was possible for the therapist to make a tape for her. The drawbacks of relying solely on a tape were outlined although it was seen as a useful staging process in this case and the therapist agreed to make one and bring it to the next session.

She reported great success in the two goals that she had set herself without any difficulties and with no anticipatory anxiety. She also reported that she was about to travel down to her parents the week afterwards, had obtained an AA route planner, and had told her mother not to offer to pick her up.

Hypnosis can help reduce the fear and anxiety caused by phobias. Here a hypnotherapist works with a woman to relieve her anxiety over taking tests. (**AP Images**)

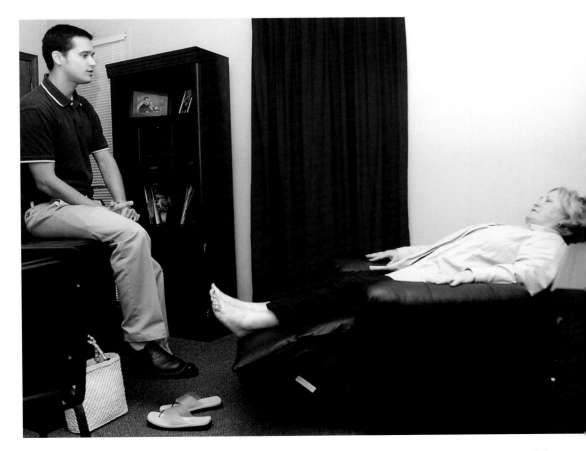

The treatment given in session 3 followed the basic pattern of the tape recording made by the therapist, and focused on the use of the special place either as somewhere to go to relax and clear her thoughts, or as somewhere to go to achieve a goal or solve a problem. In both cases it was suggested that the client lie down and look at the sky. In the first instance she should focus simply on the clear blue sky with unwanted thoughts quickly moving past like clouds. In the second it was suggested that the client visualize the goal that she was trying to achieve and to say a suitable word, for example 'success' as she visualized this. She reported that this session resulted in a very deep level of hypnosis and she was clearly very pleased at being able to deal with unwanted thoughts in a way that she usually found extremely difficult.

The final session was a review and closing session. She reported that she had achieved her goal and was feeling confident enough to continue her progress without any further sessions.

Conclusion

She made rapid progress in achieving her goal of driving by car without undue anxiety. Her motivational state and determination to achieve her goals was high and this helped the therapeutic outcome considerably. Her experience of hypnosis was both positive and powerful and although she has been unable to practise self-hypnosis the recording of a tape should help her to work towards this in the longer term. Her difficulties were formulated in terms of heightened self-consciousness following a series of dramatic accidents. The hypnosis focused on reducing these negative evaluations while at the same time allowing her to imagine a successful outcome to her driving. This, allied to her determination, meant that she was able to undertake driving tasks that she had been avoiding for some time quickly and with a minimum of anxiety.

Virtual Reality Can Cure a Fear of Driving

**David Walshe, Elizabeth Lewis,
Kathleen O'Sullivan, and Sun I. Kim**

The authors of this article are affiliated with University College Cork and St. Stephens Hospital in Cork, Ireland, and Hangyang University in Seoul, Korea. In this article they describe their experiments with virtual reality to see if it is effective in helping patients overcome the fear of driving. They discuss their efforts to make the virtual reality as realistic as possible. This included using a large-screen projection, allowing the patients to view the screen through an automobile windshield while seated in an automobile seat, and using sound effects to simulate vibration. After testing eleven patients the authors conclude that the virtual reality exposure therapy is an effective and inexpensive treatment for patients who have developed a phobia after a traffic accident.

SOURCE: David Walshe, Elizabeth Lewis, Kathleen O'Sullivan, and Sun I. Kim, "Virtually Driving: Are the Driving Environments 'Real Enough' for Exposure Therapy with Accident Victims? An Explorative Study," *CyberPsychology and Behavior*, vol. 8, 2005, pp. 532–37. Copyright © 2005 Mary Ann Liebert, Inc. Reproduced by permission.

There are few controlled studies on treatments for driving phobia. A number of case reports have suggested that systematic desensitisation is effective in treating driving fears. Other case reports and an uncontrolled case series, showed that combinations of in vivo and imaginal exposure were beneficial in driving phobia. There is a small, but growing body of case studies/case series studies supporting the role of computer generated environments in exposure therapy for driving phobia, both with motor vehicle accident (MVA) victims and with non-accident-related cases. Computer-simulated environments have used virtual reality (VR) environments and computer game environments, "game reality" (GR).

In a recent study conducted by the authors on a cohort of patients with driving phobia post-MVA, referred from the Accident and Emergency Department of a general hospital undertook an assessment for VR exposure therapy. Simulated environments involved engaging in VR driving using a head-mounted display (HMD) with tracking and thereafter driving without a HMD or tracker sitting before a 17" computer monitor for driving games which approximated driving situations and permitted setting up graded virtual driving tasks of increasing complexity and threat. In both situations driving was by means of a steering wheel with accelerator/brake pedals. This simulation was effective for 7/14 subjects who immersed into these driving environments and thereafter successfully engaged in exposure therapy. The treated group showed a marked reduction in driving phobia severity, as measured on the Fear of Driving Inventory, in PTSD severity rating and in depression severity rating. Further analysis of driving fears showed marked reductions in all areas related to vehicular travel, including travel distress, travel avoidance, and maladaptive driving strategies.

Exposure as theorised by Foa and Mc Nally must induce a level of anxiety that allows for the extinction of

A woman wears a virtual reality helmet while participating in a therapy session to treat her phobia. (© Bob Mahoney/The Image Works)

the conditioned response and the emotional processing of that experience. The synergistic relationship between presence and anxiety has been investigated, showing that for phobic subjects, increasing a sense of presence increases anxiety and increasing stress levels increases presence. Difficulties are often encountered in Imaginal Exposure to induce anxiety when imagining a feared stimulus for phobic subjects. Similar difficulties can arise in virtual environments when the subject does not immerse and the experience is not "real enough" to induce anxiety. In our initial treatment study, 7/14 patients did not immerse to the driving environments. For these patients, the environments did not induce heightened anxiety and presence and therefore were unsuitable for exposure therapy. This set a limitation to our use of VR exposure therapy as a treatment modality for driving phobia.

Virtual Reality Is Used to Treat Driving Fears

The aim of this study was to devise a VR driving treatment paradigm which would achieve an immersion/presence rate of >80%. We chose the figure of >80% as one that would be clinically acceptable to both patients and therapists when screening subjects for therapy. We used similar computer software and immersion methodology as in our reported treatment study with some noted differences. Notably, the HMD presentation was omitted from this study and some patients undertook the driving simulation as passenger. For this reason and because patients were not randomly assigned to treatment paradigms, any conclusions drawn from comparing studies must be tentative.

Eleven consecutive patients referred from the Accident and Emergency Department of Cork University Hospital or from their general practitioner, post-MVA, who met DSM-IV criteria for specific phobia-driving (from semi-structured interview by one of two clinicians) were assessed for immersion/presence while engaged in driving/traveling as a passenger, on computer-generated driving environments. Whether the subject drove or travelled as passenger was determined by his/her primary travel fear. . . .

Virtual Reality Adds Realism to Computer Games

The standard paradigm used in our earlier study was replicated. A desktop 350-Mhz Pentium III processor with 256-Mb Ram and a 128-Mb ATI Radeon graphics card was used. The computer games utilized were London Racer (Davilex), Midtown Madness II (Microsoft). Both these games support driving on the left hand side of the road, which is appropriate for driving on Irish roads. Car control was by means of a Microsoft SideWinder steering wheel with force feedback and accelerator/brake foot pedals. The participant was seated on a car seat positioned on a platform with embedded (2 x 50 W) subwoofers (Aura Bass Shaker AST-1B-4). Stereo headphones were worn. The driver/passenger viewed computer generated scenes projected from a video projector (Epson EMP-51) onto a video screen. A heart rate monitor (Healthcare Technology Ltd.) was used to record heart rate for the screening assessment.

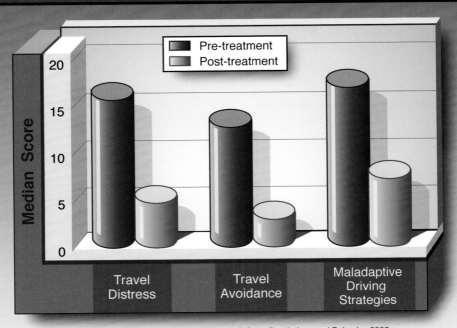

Levels of Stress Before and After Driving Therapy

Median scores of treated group on Fear of Driving Inventory (FDI).

Taken from: David Walshe et al., "Virtually Driving," *CyberPsychology and Behavior*, 2005.

The specific computer games were chosen as most suitable as their driving environments simulated "ordinary" driving environments, which included both country and city scenes with varying traffic densities allowing graded driving tasks of increasing complexity and threat. To augment the sense that the driving experience was "real," four different strategies were employed. (a) The image was projected onto a large screen (3.5 x 4 feet) using the video projector and viewed by the driver/passenger who sat behind a desk, from a distance of 6 feet. (b) A windscreen was mounted on the desk and the patient viewed the driving exposure through the windscreen. (c) A passenger seat was placed alongside the driving seat. (d) Vibration sense was augmented by more powerful subwoofers (50 watt), 25-watt subwoofers were used in the reference study. The subwoofers were attached beneath the wooden platform under the subject's feet.

The definition of immersion/presence, the software used in the driving environment and the procedure undertaken conformed closely to our earlier study. "Immersion/presence" was operationally defined as an acknowledgement by the subject that the environment "feels real," and an increase in subjective units of distress (SUD) ratings of ≥ 3 or an increase of heart rate of ≥ 15 beats per minute (BPM) while engaging in computer-simulated driving tasks of graded difficulty. Subjects were exposed to the driving environment for up to 30 min, although in some cases immersion was achieved within 2 min of driving. The virtual driving environment involved computer driving games (London Racer/Midtown Madness). These environments are not true VR environments in that it is not possible to "track" while driving. However experience demonstrates that the complexity of certain computer games including an ability to engage in realistic collisions and

FAST FACT

Hodophobia is the fear of driving.

near accident scenarios more than compensates for lack of tracking ability.

All patients were exposed to the same graded virtual driving tasks of increasing complexity and threat, as in our earlier study. If the subject's primary fear was of travelling as passenger, the therapist drove and the subject sat alongside.

The driving exposure commenced with relatively non-threatening tasks such as driving on wide roads without traffic, but if the patient failed to show evidence of immersion, the tasks gradually became more threatening, to the point where an accident situation was provoked.

Patients Take VR Seriously

Of the MVA victims, 10/11 (or 91%) with driving phobia demonstrated immersion/presence in the trial condition by (a) noting that the driving experience "feels real" and (b) feeling distressed in the driving experience or recorded increase in heart rate while driving. The same 10/11 were positive on all three measures.

Many of the patients expressed astonishment that something that they knew was not real "felt so real" and induced heightened arousal. The one patient who did not immerse found the experience amusing and commented that it was like "playing a game" and that she "couldn't take it seriously." This rate exceeds the 80%, which we proposed as clinically acceptable to both patients and therapists when screening for therapy.

None of the patients reported cybersickness during the procedure.

Making the experience "real enough" can be a problem when undertaking imaginal exposure or virtual therapy. Improving the quality of computer software both game reality (GR) and VR is one option and modifying the external environment an alternative approach. This study explored a paradigm which resulted in clinical acceptable immersion rates which, in this study, made computer-simulated driving a viable form of exposure therapy. This explorative clinical study however is not a controlled study and any conclusions drawn from comparison with the earlier study are at best tentative, as there is no valid comparative group and some procedural differences.

As in our earlier study, we took a staged approach to driving exposure, from driving on empty roads, to busy roads, to near accident situations and for one man involvement in a simulated accident was necessary to induce a sense of presence. We could not delineate how much of the 91% immersion rate was caused by the length of the immersion as opposed to the extent to which the patients confronted their fears. Our impression was that confrontation of fears was the critical feature allowing patients to activate their fear structure.

Seven of 11 patients from this sample had an overlapping diagnosis of post-traumatic stress disorder (DSM-IV diagnosis). The inclusion of these accident environments in the treatment paradigm may explain our earlier treatment success in reducing post-traumatic stress disorder (PTSD) symptom severity concurrently with reducing phobic anxiety. Exposure therapy either through imaginal exposure or eye movement desensitization and reprocessing (EMDR) has been shown to be an effective therapy for PTSD. Both therapies involve confronting the feared situations. Recent studies suggest a role for VR exposure therapy in treating PTSD. Our clinical impression is that unless the key fear of re-engaging in an accident is addressed and desensitised with emotional processing that the accident victim with driving phobia will be at high risk of developing a recurrence of illness with re-exposure to an accident situation or "near accident" situation. This impression however remains untested.

Neurolinguistic Programming Offers a Fast Cure for Phobias

Patrick Jemmer

Patrick Jemmer is a scientist at Northumbria University in Newcastle, England. In the following article he introduces Neurolinguistic Programming Fast Phobia and Trauma Cure (NLP-FP/TC), a relatively new treatment for phobias. A practitioner using the technique, Jemmer says, does not need to identify the source of the phobia but only to understand the situations in which anxieties arise. He describes the two steps of the therapy. In the first, the author says, the patient imagines watching a film of himself confronting the object of the phobia. In the second part of the therapy the patient visualizes himself rewinding the imagery—like playing a movie backward—to release the phobic fear. Jemmer reviews studies performed and concludes that NLP-FP/TC is an effective therapy for treating phobias.

T he Neuro-linguistic Programming Fast Phobia and Trauma cure (NLP-FP/TC), first described by [R.] Bandler and [S. and C.] Andreas, is a simple

SOURCE: Patrick Jemmer, Dr., "Phobia: Fear and Loathing in Mental Spaces," *European Journal of Clinical Hypnosis*, vol. 6, 2005. Copyright © 2005 by Dr. Patrick Jemmer. Reproduced by permission.

visualization that takes " . . . only a single session . . . less than fifteen minutes," according to [one expert Lee Lady] although up to three one-hour sessions may be needed, and the therapy is thus referred to as 'brief.' The NLP-FP/TC is described as a 'content free' method, as the client does not regress to infantile trauma, nor is there abreaction [the release of repressed emotions]. As Lady says: "When neutralizing a memory, the subject does not need to actually tell the therapist the details of the traumatic event." It is important to realise that as Lady explains: "The NLP phobia cure does not have to do with any particular hypotheses of what phobias are or how they arise." Rather it is sufficient to understand the situational sources of anxiety and use this understanding to help unlearn obsolete responses and relearn new ones. Indeed the NLP-FP/TC can be used to treat simple phobias as well as to neutralize memories of traumatic incidents such as abuse, combat experience, rape, and so on. An expanded example of this technique in operation is given below; this is modelled on that of Lady, who comments that "Unfortunately, since the technique is so simple I think people tend to think the brief descriptions . . . are incomplete," whereas of course exactly the opposite is true and it is the rapidity and simplicity of the intervention which is so useful! There are two steps to the NLP-FP/TC. The first step is essence Visual-Kinaesthetic Dissociation in which the client imagines (visualises) watching a film of herself confronting the object of her phobia. So, for example, with a fear of the Underground [the railway system serving the London area], then the film is not just about the Underground system, but rather it is a film of the client attempting to use the Underground and experiencing all the attendant difficulties. Moreover, the client must remain dissociated and be able to watch herself perform

FAST FACT

Neurolinguistic Programming was developed in 1976 by professors Richard Bandler and John Grinder.

the phobic response. The following extract is an example of the kind of language used and is modelled on the script given in Lady.

Patient Is Led Through a Film of Herself

Ok, now . . . imagine you're comfortable, relaxed . . . sitting in a nice warm cinema . . . that's right. . . . It's not dark. . . . Not too bright . . . get your bearings . . . have a look around. . . . Can you see where everything is . . . what it looks like . . . yes. . . . High overhead. . . . Behind you . . . is the projector. . . . The screen is clear in front of you. . . . Not too close . . . Not too far away. . . . Now I want you to imagine . . . seeing

In NLP-FP/TC treatment, clients imagine that they are sitting in a movie theater watching a film of themselves confronting the object of their phobia. (© 2008/Jupiterimages)

a black-and-white photo of yourself. . . . There . . . on the screen. . . . It's You. . . before. . . . watching a film. . . . You are going to show . . .

Yes . . . Right . . . Now. . . . But before . . . You can . . . Easily . . . Leave your body . . . Float up out of yourself. . . . Up . . . Up . . . Into the safety and warmth . . . The projection room. . . . And now you . . . Control the film. . . . So . . . now . . . In charge . . . Of the shining beam of light . . . Of the pictures on the film. . . . Yes . . . You can look far down below . . . And see . . . [name] . . . Sitting . . . Waiting . . . Watching herself . . . Comfortably waiting . . . For the film you are about to start. . . . Looking at a picture . . . Before . . .

. . . You have the experience. . . . The film is going to show . . . Good. . . . Now . . . In a moment . . . The screen is going to show a film . . . All about [name] . . . Black and white . . . yes . . . Silent. . . . This film will be in black and white. . . . There's no sound. . . . Can you even notice it flicker a bit?

And now . . . Yes . . . You have the power . . . That's right . . . To start the projector. . . . All about [name] . . . This film . . . and you watch . . . [name] . . . as she sits . . . comfortable . . . right down below . . . looking up . . . at [name] . . . there on the screen . . . just . . . watching . . . you watching [name] . . . doing some experience. . . . That's right . . . .

It can of course be very hard for the client to remain dissociated even when told just to imagine watching a film of a trauma or phobic response. It is crucial for the NLP-FP/TC that the client is dissociated. The therapist must check for appropriate dissociation by asking: 'How did you feel when you watched that film?' If the client answers 'A little bit frightened,' then the therapist should check further: 'Are you sure you were sitting in your seat . . . Watching yourself? . . . Or did you get involved in the film?' If the client has re-associated too early, then the therapist starts the visual-kinaesthetic dissociation again, using different imagery: he should be very attentive to the client's state and direct her appropriately to avoid re-association.

Phobic Memories Are Erased

The second stage of NLP-FP/TC goes as follows. The traumatic part of the film is over, and the client has observed herself doing the phobic response at several levels of dissociation. The phobic stimulus has disappeared and she is safe, secure, calm and detached. The therapist now asks the client to re-associate with the film and see, hear, smell, taste and feel all appropriate aspects of the scene. All the critical sub-modalities are turned up positively: the scene is in vivid colour and three-dimensional, for example. Then the therapist has her rewind the whole experience to the very beginning very, very fast, just like a film reel rewinding: this makes everyone walk backwards and all the images move in reverse. This process is repeated faster and faster, so that it can be done in maybe just a second. The rewinding process is repeated at this pace maybe ten times: this is the mechanism for erasing the phobic memory trace. Lady describes a modification of the Fast Phobia Cure without the rewinding. Instead, the therapist empowered the client by getting her to imagine herself as powerful and resourceful in whatever way necessary to overcome the problem presented, and this appeared to work successfully.

So, having gone to all this effort to obtain the desired outcome, how do we make sure that it 'sticks,' and produces lasting results? In the context of NLP this is done by 'future pacing.' This technique projects positive past changes forwards, thus automatically ensuring a positive future. The changes in both past and future resonate to generate the sought-after changes in the present. The therapist checks by asking, for example:

OK . . . So now . . . Imagine yourself . . . Going down the escalator . . . Down to the Underground . . . To catch the train . . . Tell me . . . Exactly how do you feel . . . How's that for you . . . Right now?

Positive Feeling Replaces Phobia

In fact, this questioning is crucial, although the precise answer is not important. A positive outcome tends to be evident from the following type of dialogue, as reported

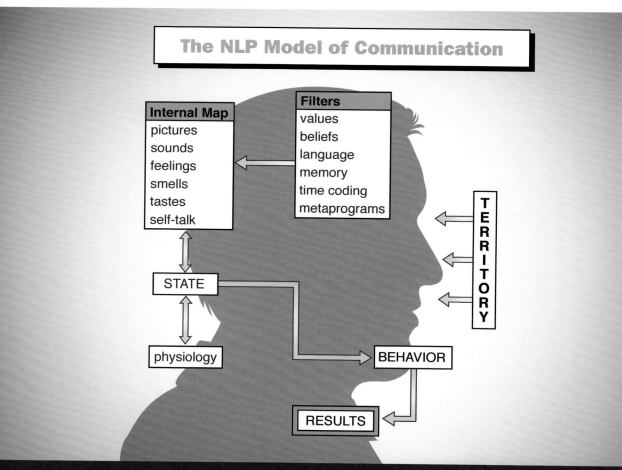

The NLP Model of Communication

Internal Map
pictures
sounds
feelings
smells
tastes
self-talk

Filters
values
beliefs
language
memory
time coding
metaprograms

TERRITORY

STATE

physiology

BEHAVIOR

RESULTS

Taken from: David Molden, *Managing with the Power of NLP*. San Francisco: Financial Times, 1996.

by Lady. "So what is the memory like for you now?" to which the answer is "I don't know. I haven't thought about it since you took me through that process. . . . I still know what happened, but it's like I read it in a book." If the response comes back as, 'Hmmm . . . just like before,' then the therapist must start the whole process again: this time different imagery should be chosen and very close attention paid to the client's physiology to make sure she is doing exactly as instructed, and eliciting the appropriate states and resources. . . .

NLP Moves to Be Effective Therapy

So, how does the NLP-FP/TC compare with other treatments? The initial part of NLP-FP/TC is in essence classic desensitisation. He says: " . . . the NLP phobia techniques are refinements of known approaches in behavioural therapy. . . . NLPers do not believe that the behavioural technique called Implosion or Flooding is the best approach for phobias, but they use a refinement of it (the Compulsion Blow-out) to break obsessions and compulsions." Thus in a behavioural approach the client learns deep relaxation which is "one of the least powerful of all internal states." Only then is she asked to imagine the phobic stimulus; trying to maintain this relaxed state under such conditions can be very hard work! The most significant difference between NLP-FP/TC and other behavioural methods is the client's sub-modal dissociation from the confrontation of the phobic stimulus in NLP-FP/TC. The client imagines watching herself doing the phobia indirectly, in a film, rather than imagining doing the phobia directly. Next the client floats 'outside herself' and watches herself watching the film; then she becomes further dissociated by becoming the projectionist who is controlling the film she is watching. She then changes the critical sub-modalities of the film itself (its colour, brightness, graininess, speed, tone, soundtrack, and so on).

Learning, Philosophizing, and Action (LPA) Technique Helps to Cure Stage Fright

Robert T. London

Robert T. London is a psychiatrist with the New York University Medical Center and the Lutheran Medical Center in New York. In this article he discusses the treatment of actors with social phobia. He describes a technique that he has pioneered called Learning, Philosophizing, and Action (LPA). London discusses the treatment of four performers—two dancers, a guitarist, and a singer—whose fears were preventing them from performing on the stage. The author describes his treatment, which begins with teaching each patient relaxation techniques. The therapy involves a combination of three treatments, London says, that the patients learn to practice by themselves. He concludes that the treatments are both flexible and effective.

Treating performers with stage fright—when the anxiety and avoidance are stressful enough to become a social phobia—is therapeutically challenging and rewarding. With our help, however, many

SOURCE: Robert T. London, MD, "Treating Stage Fright," *Clinical Psychiatry News*, vol. 34, February 2006, p. 27. Copyright © 2006 International Medical News Group. Reproduced by permission.

patients suffering from this disorder can learn to push beyond the phobic response and go on to perform magnificently.

Many times, *Diagnostic and Statistical Manual*, 4th ed. (DSM-IV) designations are not helpful when it comes to treating patients. But I have found that approaching this problem within the confines of the DSM-IV is therapeutically rewarding.

A Balanced Therapeutic Approach Works Best

The origins of phobias vary for each patient. The genetic model, the learned model, and the psychoanalytic approach all improve our understanding of phobias. The strategy that best conquers stage fright, in my experience, is the learning, philosophizing, and action (LPA) technique, which I developed at the short-term psychotherapy program at New York University Medical Center, in New York. The experiences of four show business people whom I've treated—two dancers, a guitarist, and a singer—illustrate this very well.

None of these patients had underlying depression or a generalized anxiety disorder, nor were they substance abusers. All four performers also had one problem in common: an irrational fear of going onto the stage to perform. In each case, their dreadful, irrational thoughts had different origins.

Using the LPA technique—in which you review the different concepts of phobia development, question why the fear developed, and then proceed to an action-based strategy—proved very helpful in all four cases.

Stage Fright Impacts Performers' Livelihood

Of the two dancers, one had the constant thought that she was overweight; the other had fallen while performing and, as a result, worried about falling again. In evaluating the

Stage fright is the fear of performing in front of an audience. The LPA technique can help people overcome their stage fright. (Vanessa Berberian/ Photographer's Choice/ Getty Images)

dancer who felt she was overweight, it was clear that she had no underlying mental issues about weight. She had participated in extremely physically demanding work on stage. But during some segments of her performances, she danced behind a transparent curtain—which she believed showed her weight in a negative light.

She became concerned about her "show business image," which gave her an irrational fear of performing. Further, thoughts of getting older often were on her mind before performances, which led to anxiety. As the

PERSPECTIVES ON DISEASES AND DISORDERS

years went by, she became less able to perform. In her treatment, the philosophizing part of LPA was as important as the later action phase.

The guitarist worried that he would lose his concentration and make errors, showing his group in a bad light. Those mistakes, he feared, would lead to fewer club dates.

The singer, who had once vomited on stage, was obsessed with getting sick.

In all four cases, the key issue was paralysis from irrational anxiety and fear, which prevented them from doing what they had to do to earn their living: perform on stage. Sometimes, when they forced themselves to perform, the anxiety went away; at other times, however, it did not. When a patient's phobic response leads to anxious states and possible avoidant behavior, clear thinking is hampered—and that, in turn, leads to errors or no shows. So each performer sought help.

Performers' Phobias Stem from Different Causes

Two of the patients' phobic responses had a direct relationship to the world of action. The dancer who had fallen and the singer who had become ill on stage had learned to be phobic. Directly learned phobias are the simplest to address. The learning phase and the action phase of LPA were critical to treatment for them.

The other two patients' phobic problems were more in the world of perspective. For the weight-obsessed dancer and the guitarist who feared losing concentration, the philosophizing and action phases of the LPA were the focus of their treatment.

Taking a good history and focusing on the nature of the patient's precise request for assistance—along with using sound clinical judgment focused on the problem—make for a good short-term behavior modification approach to resolving social phobias.

Whether the LPA technique, other behavioral methods, or medication is used, the focus on relieving the presenting problems is more critical than in other techniques that try to address "deeper" meanings. Those traditional techniques not only "tear down the house but the whole town as well," as a friend I've quoted in a previous column has said. Clearly, tearing down the entire town would be a drastic step in treating a social phobia.

The Therapy Is Customized to Each Patient's Needs

In the action phase of treatment for these four patients, I used a modified systematic desensitization program, developed by Dr. Joseph Wolpe, combined with in vitro flooding and reciprocal inhibition. I have found that combining and modifying these three methods give me the best results in the action phase of LPA.

First, the patient relaxes comfortably in a chair. Then she is taught a simple relaxation technique: Take a few deep breaths; slowly inhale and exhale. Usually in a few moments, the patient finds herself in a restful state, able to concentrate on specific thoughts.

After the patient comes out of the restful stage, I engage her in a conversation about her problem, focusing on the learning and philosophizing aspects of the phobia. I instruct the patient to again reenter the relaxed state, this time doing it by herself or with only a little help. In this way, the patient learns the relaxation technique on her own and will be able to use it long after leaving the treatment setting.

Once the patient is in the relaxed state, I have her visualize a large movie screen. I ask her to project herself on this screen, approaching the phobic situation— her performance anxiety. The patient should get closer and closer to the phobic situation, really seeing it on the screen but not truly experiencing it.

The patient is leading herself into a hierarchy of desensitizations that begin to help extinguish the phobia. I add another technique in which the patient can switch the screen to a pleasant experience and take a break from the phobic scene if she wishes. This adds a reciprocal inhibition segment to the treatment program.

Three Techniques Are Combined into One

The patient repeatedly watches the phobic situation on the screen, with her anxiety rising and subsequently dissipating; this is called in vitro flooding. We have now combined three behavior modification techniques into

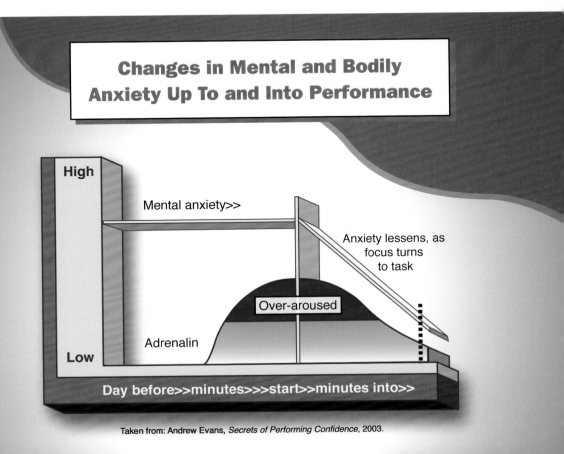

Taken from: Andrew Evans, *Secrets of Performing Confidence*, 2003.

one continuous action phase of the program. It's a triple-strategy therapy and, in my experience, leads to good results, particularly for performers, who have a unique ability to imagine and project themselves into different situations.

It also allows the patient to choose which action phase treatment she likes or finds most effective. When these techniques are used, there is rarely any stress on the patient since she realizes that she is seeing the phobic response on the screen.

Once I have worked with the patient long enough that she is able to practice this 8–10 times with me in the room, I let her decide which technique she wants to use most—or whether she'd rather work with a combination of techniques. I have the patient practice these action techniques for a minute or two 10 times a day in order to know exactly what to do when the time comes for a performance and the possibility of stage fright enters the picture.

It's important to note that I used the learning phase more for the dancer who had fallen and the vocalist who had become ill on stage.

I placed a greater emphasis on the philosophizing phase for the "overweight" dancer and the guitarist who feared losing concentration. These two had issues with perspective regarding their phobia; the previous two were linked to the world of learning, since something specific had happened.

The psychiatrist's or psychotherapist's judgment and clinical skill are used to decide what to focus on in these behavioral treatments, as is the case in determining which medication model is best for these same issues. The key is to avoid the open-ended theories of conflict and conflict resolution that may lead us to the explorative psychotherapies. Too many times, that's when the house—and the whole neighborhood—get torn down. And the phobia remains.

EMDR Helps Overcome Trauma and Other Mental Disorders

Alex Cukan

In this article from UPI, Alex Cukan explores the use of Eye Movement Desensitization and Reprocessing (EMDR) in the treatment of post-traumatic stress disorder (PTSD). A traumatic event can "get stuck" in the central nervous system and trigger a panic reaction even though there is no immediate threat. The patient identifies the negative belief, which they replace with a positive belief. Tracking eye movements that parallel those experienced in REM (rapid eye movement) sleep, the patient learns to overcome nagative and self-destructive thought patterns. In addition to PTSD, EMDR has been used in the treatment of social phobias and other mental disorders. Some practitioners have veirified the effectiveness of this treatment, while other therapists remain skeptical, and some would only recommend it in tandem with other modalities.

T o hear some mental health professionals tell it, Eye Movement Desensitization and Reprocessing is an astonishing breakthrough therapy to treat Post Traumatic Stress Disorder.

SOURCE: Alex Cukan, "Stress Treatment Offers Hope, Questions," *UPI online*, April 16, 2002. Reproduced by permission.

Created by psychologist Francine Shapiro in 1989, EMDR requires a patient to recount emotionally disturbing incidents in sequential doses while simultaneously focusing on an external stimulus. Most often, the therapist prompts the patient's eye movements, but other stimuli such as hand-tapping and aural stimulation have been used as well.

"When I first heard of EMDR from a colleague in the early 1990s, I said, 'You've got to kidding, this can't possibly work,'" Jeffrey Y. Mitchell, associate professor of the Emergency Health Services Department at the

Tracking eye movements similar to those experienced during REM sleep can help people overcome their phobias. (Allan Hobson/Photo Researchers, Inc.)

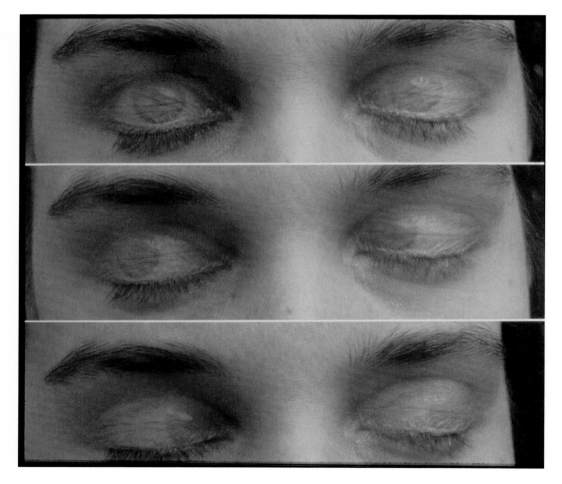

University of Maryland in Baltimore told United Press International.

"I find it nothing short of remarkable for the severely traumatized. It's dumbfounding, especially because it takes so little time in comparison with cognitive therapy, which can take months to years," Mitchell said.

Mitchell said he first used the technique with a firefighter who had not slept more than two hours a night following an episode in which he was not able to rescue three children who drowned in a car. As Mitchell prompted the eye movement, he directed the firefighter to recount the rescue attempt.

"He started to get very clear images of the sunken car and he saw that the car was pointed downward (in the water) and that he would have endangered his own life had he entered the car," Mitchell said. "I watched his face turn from pasty white to healthy pink, I saw his knees move and all kinds of body tension movements turn relaxed."

The firefighter never returned for another session because he told Mitchell, "Whatever was wrong was fixed."

EMDR can take several sessions, depending on the length and severity of the trauma, but Mitchell said the firefighter slept seven hours the night of the session and continued to sleep better in the future.

Some therapists remain skeptical, however.

"The claims of EMDR outstrip the research evidence —the research says EMDR is better than doing nothing but it is no more effective than other procedures," Scott Lilienfeld, associate psychology professor at Emory University in Atlanta, told UPI. "There's nothing magical about EMDR. It may work accidentally or it may have a placebo effect, and there's no evidence it works at a faster rate."

Robbie Dunston, coordinator of training at the EMDR Institute Inc. in Pacific Grove, Calif., said 60,000 clinicians have been trained in the two levels of EMDR.

More than 1 million people have been treated for traumas, including sexual abuse, domestic violence, combat, crime and other mental health problems.

"Only degreed and licensed mental health professionals are allowed to be trained," Dunston told UPI. "It has been used by the FBI, firefighters, rescuers, police officers and for people in war-torn countries."

Several studies have calculated the decrease in PTSD diagnoses, ranging from 80 percent to 90 percent, according to Dunston.

"I've seen police and firefighters who have been exposed to experiences causing them massive damage, and most would never work again. But my experience with EMDR is at about 90 percent," Mitchell said.

"One man drove 450 miles to thank me for mentioning a center that used EMDR in a talk I gave. He said it saved his life because he couldn't live with the PTSD any longer. I've worked at 57 major disasters, and I can say that had we not had EMDR at Oklahoma City we would have had a lot of rescuers who would have been basket cases," he added.

Several PTSD researchers were asked to comment on EMDR, and most declined. One researcher who preferred not to be identified told UPI, "The jury is split on EMDR. A lot of people are using it, and some see problems with it, and some think it will save the world."

Lilienfeld said he thought there was a gap between those who research the science of psychology and those who are practitioners. He added there was no evidence EMDR could harm a person.

Shapiro, a licensed psychologist, senior research fellow at the Mental Research Institute in Palo Alto, Calif., and executive director of the EMDR Institute said she discovered EMDR by accident in 1987 when she realized certain eye movements alleviated her own disturbing thoughts.

"Her first study with trauma victims was completed in 1989 and since then eight more studies by other researchers have shown that EMDR is effective," Dunston said.

The eye motion is believed to stimulate thinking of images of trauma "stuck" in the brain. PTSD victims, who often cannot think of such an event without strong, upsetting emotions, tend to "numb down" or avoid anything that reminds them of the trauma.

"For some reason, the images are stuck, and the person with PTSD cannot process the images. While they try not to remember them, they intrude on their thoughts," Mitchell said. "EMDR allows the person to somehow process the images and afterward remember them without the emotion."

> **FAST FACT**
>
> EMDR is most effective in treating phobias arising from traumatic events.

Shapiro admits it is not clear why EMDR works, but several theories exist. The eye movements may result in "accelerated information processing" by activating both brain hemispheres. Or, the constant sensory stimulation bombards the brain where the images are stuck. EMDR is not hypnosis, however.

Donald C. Sheehan, supervisory special agent at the FBI's Academy in Quantico, Va., said the FBI provides short-term counseling and referral and does not endorse any type of treatment. He said, however, he has seen good results from those who have sought EMDR treatment. He noted the treatment is becoming more popular among 17,000 police departments nationwide.

"What we try to do in our training is to inoculate our agents so that traumatic events are expected," Sheehan said. "We tell them that in 30 years they will fire their weapons, that people may be injured or die as a result, that everyone they know will die, that they have to expect the death of loved ones, so the way to deal with that is to treat them well while they are here."

Sheehan said the best way to cope before a traumatic event is to sleep, eat, exercise and communicate, which also is the best way to work through an event after the fact.

"The best defense to survive the trauma of a gunshot wound is to be fit, so exercise is important. During the stress of trauma, blood does not go into the stomach, so a person needs to make sure that they eat—basically we say that they should follow the advice we all got in kindergarten—eat right, sleep well and exercise."

With proper training and proper lifestyle choices, Sheehan believes PTSD can be kept to a minimum— occuring in less than 10 percent of those experiencing a severe trauma.

"This is only my opinion, but I believe the small number of people who end up with PTSD, as opposed to those that only temporarily have PTSD-like symptoms, would benefit from a wide variety of treatment modalities," he said. "I do not believe we should limit the treatment to EMDR if there is clearly a full fledged case of PTSD. That is not saying EMDR is useless. As a matter of fact, I think it should be used, just not exclusively."

Vitamins and Supplements Calm Reactions to Social Phobias

Lorie Parch

Lorie Parch, a writer for *Natural Health* magazine, describes the benefits and risks of diet supplements in the treatment of anxiety disorders. She notes that many people suffer from mild anxiety conditions and that 19 million Americans experience severe symptoms. Parch cites authorities who recommend dietary supplements, noting that in some cases these supplements should be a complement to medically supervised treatments. According to the authorities Parch cites, anxiety and tension can often be relieved with good diet and exercise. Parch then provides information about eight botanical supplements that can ease the symptoms of anxiety disorders.

A s Freud said, "The act of birth is the first experience with anxiety." For many of us, feelings of distress remain constant companions: About 19 million Americans suffer from serious anxiety conditions like

SOURCE: Lorie Parch, "Antidotes to Anxiety: Here's Our Guide to 8 Calming Supplements That Can Soothe a Fretful Mind," *Natural Health*, vol. 35, July/August 2005, pp. 95–98. Copyright © 2005 Weider Publications. Reproduced by permission.

obsessive-compulsive disorder and social phobia, reports the National Institute of Mental Health, while virtually everyone else deals with less debilitating but still harmful levels of anxiety.

Dietary Supplements Help Overcome Anxiety

Relief is as close as your supplement shelf. "There are many manifestations and degrees of anxiety," says David Bunting, director of botanical and regulatory affairs at Herb Pharm, an herbal remedy company in Williams, Ore. "My tendency would be to use botanical dietary supplements for any degree—but in severe cases only as a medically supervised complement to appropriate treatment."

Certain supplements are best taken for a limited duration. "For something that's short-term—say, anxiety related to an exam or an illness—kava and valerian are good options," says Cathy Wong, N.D., a Boston-based naturopathic doctor and About.com's alternative-medicine expert. "But they're not good for managing long-term anxiety, like a high-stress job."

Remedies for ongoing, generalized anxiety always circle back to lifestyle solutions. Regular workouts and a balanced diet that contains adequate amounts of magnesium and B vitamins can do a world of tension-relieving good. "One of my first recommendations for someone who has a lot of anxiety is aerobic exercise, as well as calming exercise like yoga or tai chi," Wong says. Both types will help stave off the burnout caused by chronically elevated levels of the stress hormone cortisol.

For occasional anxiety, try these supplements, which may soothe a temporarily troubled mind.

B Complex

A good first step in relieving anxiety. "B vitamins are essential for stress management, energy production, and neurotransmitter health," says Cathy Wong, N.D. Helpful supplements usually include vitamins [B.sub.1] (thiamin), [B.sub.2] (riboflavin), [B.sub.3] (niacin), [B.sub.5] (pantothenic acid), [B.sub.6] (pyridoxine hydrochloride), [B.sub.9] (folic acid), and [B.sub.12] (cyanocobalamin).

Cautions. B vitamins are very safe. Thiamin may turn urine bright yellow, and niacin may cause flushing—both are harmless side effects.

Use of Herbal Medicines in Primary Care Patients, by Psychiatric Diagnosis

Taken from: *Psychosomatics*, 46: 117–22, April 2005.

Dosage. Wong recommends taking a daily B-50 supplement, which offers 50 milligrams each of most B vitamins, along with 400 micrograms of folic acid.

GABA

Gamma-aminobutyric acid has a calming effect on the brain, working similarly to the tranquilizers Valium and Xanax. "This nonessential amino acid blocks stress and anxiety by preventing neurons from overfiring," explains Wong.

Cautions. Possible side effects include nausea (especially in doses over 3 grams per day), shortness of breath, and tingling in the hands and face.

Dosage. Wong suggests a daily dose of 500 mg to 3 grams per day.

Kava

Kava, or *Piper methysticum*, is traditionally used in its native Polynesia to increase sociability and mild euphoria. Herb Pharm's David Bunting calls it "the most specific and effective herb for anxiety." It can be especially useful in anxiety-related cases of asthma, high blood pressure, PMS, insomnia, and as a muscle relaxant. Research in the journal *Psychopharmacology* has shown it to be more effective than a placebo in non-psychotic anxiety disorders.

Cautions. Liver damage is a potential risk, so anyone with liver conditions or Parkinson's disease shouldn't take kava; neither should anyone using alcohol, benzodiazepines, or other depressants. Kava is a short-term treatment. "Using it for three or more months has been associated with dry skin, pulmonary hypertension, shortness of breath, and eye redness," warns Wong.

Dosage. About 40 drops of tincture up to four times a day, or capsules up to three times daily, according to instructions. Look for capsules with 60 mg total kavalactones, advises Bunting. Discuss any kava regimen with your physician.

Magnesium

This essential mineral helps ease muscle tension, anxiety, and stress. A 2004 study published in *Current Medical Research and Opinion* found that magnesium taken with hawthorn and California poppy extracts was both safe and effective in treating patients with mild-to-moderate anxiety disorder, says James Gormley, co-author of *The User's Guide to Brain-Boosting Supplements.*

Cautions. The most common side effect of magnesium supplementation is loose stools, says Wong. The mineral may also interfere with the efficacy of ACE inhibitors, diabetes medication, or tetracycline. Women taking birth control pills or hormone replacement therapy may need to increase magnesium to see a calming effect.

Dosage. Gormley and Wong both suggest 200 to 300 mg two times a day; you may need to experiment with the dosage based on side effects. Food sources of magnesium include kelp, wheat bran and germ, almonds, cashews, collard greens, and blackstrap molasses.

Passionflower

Dried passionflower (*Passiflora incarnata*) can relieve stress, anxiety, and insomnia, says Gormley. In a double-blind study in the *Journal of Clinical Pharmacy and Therapeutics,* giving patients with generalized anxiety disorder 45 drops per day of passionflower tincture was effective in reducing symptoms without impairing job performance (unlike the anti-anxiety drug Serax, also part of the study).

Cautions. Generally considered very safe, passionflower can cause drowsiness and should not be used by anyone taking anti-depressants or anti-anxiety medication.

> **FAST FACT**
>
> A recent study showed that as many as 42 percent of the U.S. population have used herbs and dietary supplements, with anxiety and depression being the leading reasons.

Dosage. Available in tincture, tea, or capsule form, sometimes mixed with valerian and lemon balm (*Melissa officinalis*). Use 40 drops of tincture up to five times a day, says Bunting; Wong recommends 400 mg divided over the day.

Relora

A man buys dietary supplements at a vitamin store. The anxiety of phobias may be reduced by taking certain supplements. **(AP Images)**

This patented formula combines extracts from magnolia bark (*Magnolia officinalis*) and the amur corktree (*Phellodendron amurense*), both used in Traditional Chinese Medicine. "Magnolia bark contains two compounds, magnolol and honokiol, which are believed to be responsible for the stress-reducing effects," says Wong. Relora seems to work on some of the same receptors as anti-anxiety drugs without causing sedation.

Cautions. If you're pregnant, nursing, or taking prescription drugs, consult your doctor before using Relora.

Dosage. Most company research on Relora has looked at a regimen of 250 mg, three times a day, taken with food.

Rescue Remedy

British physician Edward Bach designed this formula to be used in times of acute emotional stress. It blends five flower essences: star of Bethlehem (for shock), clematis (for inattentiveness), impatiens (for irritation and impatience), cherry plum (for irrational thoughts), and rock rose (for panic).

Cautions. One of the strengths of Rescue Remedy is that it doesn't interact with medications, says Wong. It is at its most effective in relieving short-term acute anxiety rather than chronic anxiety.

Dosage. Available as an extract or spray. Place four drops of the extract in the mouth four times a day, or as needed; add the drops to water and sip, or rub on the lips. Two quick sprays have the same effect.

Valerian

The mild sedative qualities of *Valeriana officinalis* come from its roots and rhizomes. "Valerian is used in treating sleep disorders to shorten the time to enter sleep and to improve sleep quality," says Bunting. "It's also used for anxiety, especially nervous anxiety, mental strain, agitation, muscle spasms, stress, and stress-related headaches and muscle tension." The plant likely works by accelerating the release of gamma-aminobutyric acid, explains Gormley. A 2002 study in *Phytotherapy Research* found that valerian was as effective as Valium in reducing anxiety.

Cautions. The use of fresh valerian has little, if any, side effects, though Bunting cautions that taking the dried herb for more than three months may result in headaches and restlessness. Avoid the herb entirely if you have a liver condition or if you're taking any drug that depresses the central nervous system, including alcohol.

Dosage. As much as 40 drops of tincture up to five times a day, or a 300 to 400 mg capsule twice a day. "If you have anxiety-associated sleep problems, take one capsule in the early evening and the other 30 minutes to one hour before bed," advises Wong. Dried valerian may be used as a tea, but many people dislike its strong odor.

CHAPTER 3

The Personal Side of Phobias

Panic Attack Leads to Phobic Avoidance

Anonymous

This author of this account describes how a panic attack led to her social phobia, and the effect it had on her life. Her anxiety about leaving the house became so severe she began to fear something horrible happening every time she would venture out and be in public. The turning point came when she realized she was not "going insane" but had a medical condition, and her determination to live a normal life again prompted her to seek medical help.

M y life seemed to be coming apart at the seams, right before my eyes: everything that could go wrong seemed to be going wrong, and I felt completely powerless to change any of it. Marital issues, a death in the family, financial problems. I was horrified that anyone would discover what a mess I felt like or that I even had any problems. For the outside world my life was relatively perfect: my husband and I owned our own

Photo on previous page. Phobias can have a profound effect on a person's life.
(Paolo/Plainpicture/ Jupiterimages)

SOURCE: Stephen Pravel, "Bree's Story" from *PanicCare.org.* 2008. Copyright © by Dr. Stephen Pravel. Reproduced by permission. http://www.paniccare.org/id32.html.

business, had a beautiful daughter, were living in Birmingham, great social life. But I knew the truth, I was a disaster just like my life felt—the business was fledgling, my marriage on the rocks, we could hardly afford the payments on the house. I simply could not deal with anything, but I simply could not tell anyone that.

An agoraphobic woman looks out the window. Agoraphobia is a morbid fear of public places or open spaces. **(David Gifford/Photo Researchers, Inc.)**

Stress Brings on Panic Attack

My lip glossed smile and manicured nails hid all the hurt and fears from the outside world of my coming undone . . . then all of a sudden—SNAP—like being hit by a runaway train, my head felt as if it were full of swarming bees, buzzing with crazy thoughts at 75 mph on the expressway . . . my fingers began to tingle with numbness, my breath quick and shallow, my throat constricting so that I could hardly swallow. I was trembling from head to toe, my heart beating out of my chest, head spinning with dizziness and I was so hot, on fire I felt—I just knew I was going to die. Stroke. Heart attack. Seizure. I could not get to my exit fast enough, time seemed to stand still. I am going to die right here, right now, was all I could think and in the meantime kill others as my car catapults out of control. I could not reach my destination fast enough. As I finally exited the highway after what seemed like years, the physical symptoms began to dissipate and the horrible thoughts were replaced with thoughts of having escaped a dire situation and now I am safe . . . but I must be going insane! What was that?

Exhausted and drained I arrived at my home and felt so safe: so safe indeed, that the very next day when I needed to run an errand, I began thinking of the previous day's events and began thinking "what if" thoughts . . . what if *that* happens again? As I regretfully pulled out of my driveway, my thoughts raced and became incomprehensible . . . what if I just die right in the store or have a stroke and fall on the floor and kill myself, or I just go suddenly blind? Just like that, in the blink of an eye—die, blind, debilitated. I, like a madwoman, raced through the store tossing items into my cart as quickly as I could, with only the thought of getting home and being safe again in my mind. The physical symptoms began again . . . my hands trembled so much, simply signing my

FAST FACT

The word *phobia* is derived from Phobos, the ancient Greek god of fear.

credit card receipt was embarrassing (someone could see I was anxious), which, of course, began new thoughts of loss of motor skills, etc. I began to associate leaving the house and being in public as a threat—something horrible or tragic would surely become of me or my "problem" would be discovered.

Fear of Panic Attacks Leads to Avoidance

Having a family and pets to care for precluded me from not leaving the house again as I wished, but I did so with dread and [resignation]. This continued for months and months, dealing with the thoughts and issues associated with my feelings, I proceeded to have more "attacks", mostly in situations where I felt I had limited or no escape. I began to avoid each and every situation where an attack had occurred, fearing that encountering the situation again would bring about another awful, horrible attack. Boulevard turns, the Up escalator, 4 lane roads, etc. The fear of leaving my home, driving, the stray thoughts of dropping dead, strokes, blindness, loss of motor skills would always lead to an "attack" and I would consequently avoid that specific situation again. Eventually, the few stores and places I visited regularly became safe places but not without having extreme anxiety while driving to them. But I swore I would never, never drive on the highway again. NEVER! Nor any other situation where an "attack" had occurred.

Searching for a Solution

I began researching my symptoms online, knowing they were irrational and obviously not predicting any misfortune. I was so sick of being sick! I found that I was experiencing anxiety and/or panic disorder—not going insane. But this did not, however, make the avoided situations any better and I continued to have anxiety daily about leaving my home, driving, potentially being put in a panic inducing situation. Eventually, I had a few places within a mile of my house that I could go to "safely", but my life and work did not permit me the exclusiveness of these locations. Traveling outside my safety zone generally led to a panic attack and subsequently I would avoid that situation again . . . leaving me sometimes driving miles and miles out of my way to simply avoid a particular intersection or turn. The ever looming threat of an attack and the avoidance of almost all driving situations took its toll on every aspect of my life. I was horrified someone would discover my feelings. I was so ashamed of the way I felt. Fed up, crying almost daily, living in constant fear of some tragic event befalling me, I finally decided I truly needed outside help.

Virtual Reality Offers Relief from Fear of Flying

Kathy Feldman

Kathy Feldman, the author of this selection, was a patient who suffered from fear of flying. She describes how her phobia developed after a frightening sightseeing trip in a small general aviation aircraft. She tells how her fear ultimately forced her to give up flying and the strain it placed on her family. After noting other therapies she had tried, the author explains how virtual reality helped to overcome her fears. She concludes by offering helpful insights into ways to cope with the fear of flying.

By the time I decided to do Virtual Reality Therapy I had done most everything else I could possibly do that was offered. I had done:

• Cognitive Therapy

• Biofeedback

• Hypnosis

• EMDR

• A Fear of Flying Clinic

SOURCE: Kathy Feldman, "Virtual Reality Therapy and How It Helped," *VRPhobia.com*, 2001. Reproduced by permission.

Fear of Flying Starts with Bad Experience

At the time, the closest Virtual Reality Medical Office to my home was in San Diego, an eleven-hour car ride away. I had never had a problem flying until 1994, when my family and I boarded a small, general aviation plane for a tour over the Grand Canyon. While the plane was built for a fewer amount of people, we were packed into it like sardines. The plane ride was an hour's worth of bumps, hits and jolts. It felt like the plane wanted to drop

This image is seen by participants in a virtual reality therapy session for fear of flying. (© Bob Mahoney/The Image Works)

out of the sky under the weight of its many passengers and I was in a blind panic the entire time. It was this experience that imprinted a bad belief system and distorted view of flying in my head.

When the plane finally touched down, I got out of the plane and kissed the ground. Literally, the first words that came out of my mouth were "My life has been changed forever" and for seven years, that statement was true. While I continued to fly after that incident, it was never the same. For instance, when I had travel plans that involved flying, I would begin having anticipatory anxiety about three weeks before the scheduled flight. I would lose sleep. I would have nightmares. I would obsess about the flight.

My mind couldn't think about anything else BUT the flight. My thought process would be filled with "what if's." It was so bad that by the time the day of travel came around, I emotionally didn't have anything left over for the actual flight. My desire and drive and inner-strength for flying were completely zapped and spent. There was nothing emotionally left over for me to push through the actual flight. I felt paralyzed by the fear.

On one occasion, after I had boarded a plane with my two children and just before the Flight Attendant closed the door to the aircraft, I bolted off the plane leaving my children behind to fly on without me. I will never forget the tears and look of disappointment on their faces. At that point, I stopped flying all together for a number of years. I was exhausted and I was tired of putting my family through this unforgiving process each and every time we wanted to fly someplace.

Virtual Reality Provides Freedom from Fear

Then, I found Virtual Reality Therapy. For me, because of the nature of the feedback I received during the VRT sessions, I was able to identify my "flying rough spots" easier. Virtual Reality Therapy gave me more concrete feedback about what I, as a nervous flyer, needed to work through to begin flying again. Because the "fear" had this "invisible hold" on me, Virtual Reality Therapy gave me a realistic and physiological perspective about myself that I could grasp and wrap my mind around so that I could actually understand what it was I needed to do to progress. Working yourself out of fear to the point where you can fly without anxiety or panic is a process that is unique to each person. Whatever you do, don't stop trying —even if it seems nothing is working. In the long run, it will all pay off.

First, you need to be committed to finding a "cure" for yourself. Fear of flying is the type of thing that will creep back into your life if you don't keep it in check. Therefore, don't fly less because of the fear, FLY MORE! Fly as often as you possibly can. By flying more, you will be giving yourself a chance to purge your old belief system. By flying more, you will be giving yourself the chance to put your new belief system into place. By flying more, you will be able to prove to yourself that the old belief system simply doesn't work any longer.

Planning Ahead Takes Fear Out of Flying

Take all the "decision making" out of flying beforehand. Do whatever you can "pre-flight" to prepare so that on the day of your flight, all the choices and decisions surrounding flying are done. There's nothing worse for a nervous flier than to have to make even the simplest decisions and/or choices on the day of travel. The nervous flier's mind is simply too balled up in fear at that point. For example:

1. The night before you travel, lay out the clothing you will be wearing on your flight.

2. Be absolutely packed by the day before travel, including your Bag of Tricks, which may include:

- MP3 player packed with your favorite music
- Bottled water
- Battery powered fan
- Inspiration index cards
- Pictures of loved ones
- Reading materials

FAST FACT

Fear of flying may be caused by other fears such as loss of control, confinement, or heights.

3. Allow yourself plenty of time to get to the airport and checked in at the gate.

4. Once at the airport, take a more positive cue from fellow travelers. Look around and notice how everybody is just going about their own business, without fear. Being around other travelers can put your "distorted view of flying" back into perspective.

5. Once you have boarded, let the Flight Attendant know you are a nervous flier and ask to be checked on from time to time.

6. Now that most airplanes have sky phones on them, arrange for a family member or friend to stay by the telephone while you are in flight. If you feel restless or out-of-sorts, use the sky phone to call that person. It is a very calming thing to do.

7. Ask the Flight Attendant if you can meet the pilots. Talk with the Pilots about anything that's on your mind. Pilots and Flight Attendants are the nicest and most helpful people. Remember, the airline industry wants your business. To get it, though, they must first earn your trust and respect—and they do this by wanting to make your flight comfortable. It's OK to lean on them.

Loss of Control Leads to Fear of Flying

Anonymous

In this anonymous selection "Kathryn" discusses her fear of flying and explores the impact it has had on her life. She notes that she was not always afraid to fly. In fact, she says she enjoyed hot-air ballooning and skydiving even though the flight up was a problem. Kathryn shares her belief that the root of her fear is most likely a feeling of loss of control. The catalyst, she says, was a flight in a four-seat Cessna. The author explains how a combination of behavioral therapy and a low dose of antianxiety medication helped her return to the skies again.

"Ok enough, Kathryn. Stop squeezing my arm! You must stop this nonsense," my older sister sternly told me, aboard a short flight home from North Carolina. I willed myself to loosen my grip. Deep breaths. The plane wasn't falling, it wasn't shaking violently, and there was hardly a cloud in the sky.

I snuck a one-eyed peek out the window and reminded myself that the plane was just leveling off. Even so, as the pilot pulled back on the throttle, I tried to contain my panic and suppress thoughts of engine failure.

Fear of Flying Developed in Adulthood

I wasn't always filled with an irrational fear of flying. When I was little, I loved looking from planes and seeing tracts of rural farmland perfectly assembled like little puzzle pieces. I tried to guess the distance to the horizon, look for familiar landmarks on approach to Washington, and take long naps. In recent years, however, I more typically found myself staring intently down at the pages of book, never truly able to read it.

My fear of flying wasn't that extreme. I could still make myself take trips (except for the one time I flat out canceled a trip to San Diego to visit a friend, on the day I was scheduled to leave, because of forecasted storms). I never totally flipped out, and you'd probably never know the thoughts racing through my mind, or know my heart rate was soaring, if you sat next to me on a plane. It's totally foolish, I know. It's definitely a personal problem, which makes it all the more difficult for me to explain and for my friends/family to understand.

I had aviation hobbyists and even a career airline pilot give me lessons in physics and jet propulsion, which never helped. It especially didn't help when the pilot asked me what part of flying scared me the most, and I replied without hesitation, "Definitely, take off." He responded incredulously, "Take off?! Well. Let me tell you, you should be way more scared of landing. It's far more difficult." Nor did it help when people cite statistics of how improbable it would be for my flight to be the doomed one. In my mind, it's just one bolt that pops in the wing or tail . . . and poof. I prefer to think of my phobia as more of a case of an overactive imagination, namely of what the pilot might know that I don't.

For some, takeoff is the most terrifying part of flying. (**Mason Morfit/Workbook Stock/ Jupiterimages**)

Fear of Flying Does Not Stop Skydiving and Ballooning

Let's back up . . . when did this all start? The events of 9/11 are often cited as a trigger for some people's fear of air travel. Terrorism on planes isn't what scares me the most (I happen to think that ticketing counters and those long, snaking security lines are more likely targets). Ask me why I willingly went skydiving last year, and even stranger, why the scariest part was the flight up (really!!). Ask me why I loved hot air ballooning in the Rocky Mountains on a windy day, and never wanted to come down. I will say that I've never liked uncontrollable circumstances, which is most likely the root of this fear. It makes sense, given that in all of my flying dreams, I'm never at or near the controls.

I really don't know for sure what it is that made me question the mechanics of flight, or what convinced me planes are simply way too heavy to be in the air and even more miraculously, stay suspended for hours at a time. The only possible time that I can pinpoint is a short flight aboard a four-seater Cessna I took a few years ago. I wasn't scared at the time . . . but I know I wasn't scared before, and I've been a nervous flyer ever since. My fear is compounded by the fact that I have recurring dreams of planes not getting off the ground, of planes losing lift while making sharp turns, and of planes simply stalling and falling. To me, in my mind at least, I believe this contributes to these imaginary scenarios becoming "real."

Therapist and Medication Conquer Fear of Flying

After the canceled trip to San Diego, I resolved to do something about it. It turns out that in addition to uncontrollable circumstances, I also dislike things that actually control me. So in fact I did two things. First, I saw a therapist, who helped me understand that although I am not prone to worry or anxiety in my every day life, it's not uncommon for people to develop fears, and specifically situational phobias, in their mid-twenties. Second, I saw my internal medicine doctor, who prescribed a low dose of a mild antianxiety medication to take before my flight. I was initially resistant to the idea of taking something, but I tried it once, and was amazed to discover that I could observe things on the flight for what they really were —the engine pulling back, light turbulence, an easy turn. I watched an inflight movie, and even found myself

> **FAST FACT**
>
> Fear of flying frequently develops in adults after a traumatic incident.

wishing I had requested a window seat so I could look out. I didn't feel drugged up; I just felt very "Whatever." I was sold. An added benefit: On another flight, when I landed and learned my checked bag had been lost, I was delighted to find that since the medication hadn't quite worn off, I really didn't mind at all.

Through learning about phobias, I've come to accept the perspective that they are often the result of something that should be exciting turning into something scary and unpredictable. My sister, with her tough-love approach, who initially told me to "Deal with it, and get over it," may have been right, if not totally sympathetic. My rational side knows that's just life . . . unpredictable, and scary, but also exciting. With a little help, I have learned to recognize this and to deal with it—a process which, I feel, has made me a stronger, calmer, and more patient person.

Specific Phobias Lead to Social Phobia

Adam S. Trotter

In this article Adam S. Trotter shares his life experiences dealing with specific and social phobias. He describes how his life changed as a young child when his family moved from England to North Carolina. His specific phobias began with a fear of thunderstorms, which he had not experienced before, and spiders. From these initial phobias, he says, he developed social phobia, as he feared embarrassing himself in public. Trotter describes how medication helped him overcome his anxiety disorders. He closes by noting that the medication that helped him can benefit others, too. All phobia sufferers, he concludes, should consult their doctors.

W hen I was born, my father was in the U.S. Air Force; before I was six months old, he, my mother and I moved to England. I learned to talk there, and to read a bit, and generally came into my human awareness in a clean, sleepy little town in

SOURCE: Adam S. Trotter, *RemedyFind Anxiety Disorders Newsletter*, 2006. Copyright © 2006 by Adam Somers Trotter. Reproduced by permission.

Oxfordshire. But when I was two and a half, my father left the military and we returned to my ancestral home in North Carolina. Suddenly I was surrounded by strange-acting, strange-talking people who were my cousins and aunts and grandparents. The food was strange, the trees were strange, but strangest of all were the thunder and the spiders.

I'm sure there were occasional thunderstorms in England, and certainly there were spiders. My favorite song, learned over there, was "Itsy-bitsy Spider Climbed up the Water Spout." But nothing could prepare me for a North Carolina summer. Thunderstorms are practically an everyday experience, and they can be severe. And the spiders were bigger—much bigger—and seemed to be hiding in every corner. One of my earliest memories of that time is sitting in a spider-infested rowboat in the middle of a pond, a distant thunderhead rumbling closer, while my grandfather showed me how to spear live worms on a hook and reel in bloody fish. If I ever write a horror novel, that will be the place where I start.

I was a curious child, and of course I asked what the thunder was. I don't remember who I asked, but I vividly remember the answer: "Thunder is clouds butting heads." So now, on top of the startling bang and ominous rumble of thunder, I had to deal with the alarming image of great cloud-beasts bellowing and charging at each other, waging titanic wars right over my head. The only safe spot was in the arms of my parents, and I would go to reckless extremes, tumbling down stairs, to reach that refuge in the short time between the flash of lightning and the dreaded thunder.

Fear of Spiders Leads to Blind Panic

Later, I learned the physics of thunder, and the panic and fear disappeared with only a nostalgic trace. But, perhaps because I was not a biologist, my fear of spiders remained, and was reinforced by unfortunate encounters

This woman suffers from arachnophobia, the fear of spiders. (Tony Hutchings/ Photographer's Choice /Getty Images)

in various spidery places. For many years into adulthood, whenever I found myself in a new place, I would conduct a compulsive survey of the local spider population. I would not sit with my legs under a table, because table spiders might threaten my knees. I would strip my bed thoroughly each night in a search for bed spiders. Boats were out of the question.

In the rare instance that a large spider did find me out, I would fly into a blind panic. I've jumped out of boats, stripped my clothes and flung myself against fences to escape. Every time, my extreme behavior left me with a profound sense of embarrassment, and an increased determination to avoid such public panic.

Medication Overcomes Phobias

Ten years ago, I began taking SSRI antidepressants, like Zoloft or Prozac, as well as benzodiazepine anti-anxiety medication, like Ativan or Klonopin. Some months after starting this new regimen, I was invited to spend a weekend in a lakeside cabin. There were spiders, the big, crunchy kind. I felt the stirrings of panic, but, to my surprise, the panic never quite materialized.

I've talked with several excellent psychiatrists about my arachnophobia. I've come to realize that, sometime in adolescence, my phobia joined forces with a more generalized social anxiety. Which came first? I don't know. But the fact is, my specific phobia blossomed into something larger: the fear of public panic.

Not all people who suffer from panic attacks suffer from specific phobias, and not all phobias lead to public panic attacks. But in a great many cases, childhood phobias result in public panic attacks—traumatic experiences that reinforce the original phobia and, more important, engender agoraphobia. Agoraphobia, the fear of being in public spaces, often supplants the original specific phobia. Suffering a public panic attack, for whatever reason, is a traumatic event. Many who suffer panic attacks say that they feel like they are dying, really dying. It's terrifying. It would not surprise me if people who've suffered panic attacks develop symptoms of post-traumatic stress disorder. After all, what is more traumatic than believing you're about to die?

The remedy: talk to your doctor about getting on SSRI antidepressants (even if you're not depressed) and benzodiazepines. It is all but impossible to have a panic attack if you are taking these medications. It takes a while to realize this, but it's true. Then, with the help of friends and family, you can begin to venture forth and confront your fears. And while you're at it, you can dust away those childhood cobwebs.

GLOSSARY

anticipatory anxiety	The fear that a panic attack will occur.
antidepressant	Drugs used to control and prevent depression and anxiety. These fall into two categories—MAO inhibitors and selective seretonin reuptake inhibitors (SSRIs).
anxiety	Uneasiness or apprehension about an impending event. Symptoms may include racing heartbeat, sweaty palms, dry mouth, and goose bumps.
beta-blockers	Medication to control irregular heartbeat in cardiac patients. Beta-blockers are also used to control panic attacks.
cognitive therapy	A therapy that was developed in the 1970s by Professor Aaron T. Beck at the University of Pennsylvania. The treatment focuses on thought patterns to overcome fears rather than addressing the historic causes of the phobia or anxiety.
conditioned response	A behavior modification therapy that involves learning new reactions in response to conditioned stimuli.
flooding	A treatment in which the patient is completely immersed in the fear response to a particular object or situation until the fear eventually fades away.
hypochondria	An anxiety disorder in which the sufferer is excessively concerned with health and may create imaginary illnesses.
implosive therapy	A form of image therapy in which the patient looks inward to visualize secure outcomes for the events that have triggered panic attacks.
MAOI	Monoamine oxidase inhibitors are a class of antidepressant drugs, which are useful in overcoming social anxieties.
modeling	A theory about the origins of phobias. This theory contends that children learn their phobias from their elders.

neurosis	A mental disorder arising for no apparent reason in which the sufferer exhibits symptoms such as anxiety, insecurity, or depression. In contrast with psychosis, the sufferer does not experience hallucinations.
panic attack	A sudden alarm in which the sufferer loses self-control and fears irrational outcomes including death.
participant modeling	A form of therapy in which the patient observes how the therapist copes with a situation and then attempts to duplicate his or her behavior.
phobia	A debilitating and irrational fear of a situation, event, object, or creature. A person with a phobia will go to extreme lengths to avoid the negative stimulus.
psychiatrist	A medical doctor (MD) who specializes in mental disorders. Doctors can prescribe medication to supplement therapy.
psychologist	A scientist who specializes in mental disorders and processes. As a specialist with a graduate degree (PhD), a psychologist can offer therapy but cannot prescribe medication.
psychosis	A mental condition in which the patient hallucinates, suffers delusions, and loses touch with reality.
repression	The process of supressing negative feelings or memories of traumatic events for an extended time, leading to anxiety and other mental problems.
selective seretonin reuptake inhibitors	Commonly referred to as SSRIs, a class of antidepressants used to treat depression, anxiety, and some personality disorders.
social phobia	An irrational fear of being with other people or in public places.
specific phobia	An irrational fear of a situation, event, object, or creature.
systematic desensitization	A form of therapy in which the patient is exposed to gradually increasing levels of the stimulus that triggers his or her phobia.

CHRONOLOGY

B.C. circa 400   Hippocrates describes a person who is excessively shy as one who "loves darkness as life" and "thinks every man observes him."

A.D. Middle Ages   Arachnophobia is traced to a fear held by Europeans who believe that spiders foretell plague and death.

1621   Robert Burton, an English minister, writes *Anatomy of Melancholy*, in which he describes people with various fears, which would be called phobias today.

1769   A. LeCamus, a French doctor, writes *Des Aversions*, a book about phobias.

1789   Benjamin Rush, an American doctor, describes phobias as "a fear of an imaginary evil, or an undue fear of a real one."

1871   Otto Westphal writes *Die Agoraphobie*, in which the term *agoraphobia* is used for the first time to describe the condition.

1894   Sigmund Freud writes "On the Grounds for Detaching a Particular Syndrome from Neurasthenia Under the Description 'Anxiety Neurosis,'" establishing anxiety neurosis as a psychiatric classification.

1896   Theodule Ribot, the founder of French psychology, writes in *Psychology of Emotions* of a "veritable deluge" of people complaining of phobias.

1960s South African–born psychotherapist Joseph Wolpe develops behavior therapy (BT) in the United States.

1962 Psychologist C. Weekes describes a panic attack as "an intense recurring spasm of panic."

1964 D.F. Klein describes a clear link between panic attacks and phobias.

1966 The first phobia organization in the world, the Open Door, is founded. It later changes its name to PAX.

1968 *The Diagnostic and Statistical Manual* of Mental Disorders second edition (DSM-II) defines social phobia as being a specific fear of being watched and examined by others.

1978 The Epidemiological Catchment Area Survey by the National Institute of Mental Health is launched to measure the incidence of mental health disorders among participants in five United States cities.

1980 The third edition of the DSM (DSM-III) provides a clinical diagnosis of social phobia.

1987 The DSM-III refines its definition of social phobia to include symptoms that cause "interference or marked distress" as opposed to "significant distress."

1990 The National Comorbidity Survey is begun to measure the incidence of mental disorders included in the DSM-III.

1994 The DSM-IV begins using "social anxiety disorder" instead of "social phobia."

ORGANIZATIONS TO CONTACT

Anxiety Disorder Association of America (ADAA)
8730 Georgia Ave., Suite 600
Silver Spring, MD 20910
(240) 485-1001
www.adaa.org

Formed in 1980, the Anxiety Disorder Association of America is a nonprofit organization that works to prevent, treat, and cure anxiety disorders. The ADAA provides information about anxiety disorders, lobbies for cost-effective treatment, and assists people in obtaining treatment for anxiety disorders.

The Anxiety Panic Internet Resource (TAPIR)
www.algy.com/anxiety

This self-help Internet resource started in 1993. The Web site is dedicated to providing information and relief to people suffering from anxiety disorders. TAPIR is unaffiliated with any organization or business. It provides an opportunity for people to interact with others who suffer from or have an interest in anxiety disorders.

Freedom from Fear
308 Seaview Ave.
Staten Island, NY 10305
(718) 351-1717
www.freedomfrom fear.org

Since 1984 Freedom from Fear has been a nonprofit mental health advocacy organization whose mission is to improve the lives of people suffering from anxiety disorders.

National Anxiety Foundation
3135 Custer Dr.
Lexington, KY 40517
www.lexington-On-line.com/naf.html

The National Anxiety Foundation is a volunteer nonprofit organization that is an advocacy group to educate both the public as well as professionals about anxiety disorders. It does so through print and electronic media.

National Institute of Mental Health
6001 Executive Blvd.,
Room 8184,
MSC 9663
Bethesda, MD 20892
(301) 443-4513
(866) 615-6464
www.nimh.nih.gov/
health/topics/anxiety
-disorders/index.shtml

The National Institute of Mental Health provides research on mental disorders. It publishes information and offers help on locating mental health services.

National Phobics' Society
Zion CRC,
339 Stretford Rd.
Hulme, Manchester
M15 4ZY UK
08444 775 774
www.phobics-society
.org.uk

Founded thirty years ago in the United Kingdom, the National Phobics' Society works to relieve suffering and to support people with anxiety disorders. It provides information and services and works with health care professionals as well as the public.

Social Phobia/Social Anxiety Association
2058 East Topeka Dr.
Phoenix, AZ 85024
www.socialphobia.org

The Social Phobia/Social Anxiety Association provides a forum for locating cognitive-behavioral therapy groups and is a resource for treatments of social phobias.

FOR FURTHER READING

Books

Edmund J. Bourne, *The Anxiety and Phobia Workbook*, 4th ed. New York: New Harbinger, 2005.

———, *Beyond Anxiety & Phobia.* New York: New Harbinger, 2001.

Carol Christensen, *Power over Panic: Answers for Anxiety.* Colorado Springs, CO: Life Journey, 2003.

Emily Ford, with Michael R. Liebowitz and Linda Wasmer Andrews, *What You Must Think of Me: A Firsthand Account of One Teenager's Experience with Social Anxiety Disorder.* New York: Oxford University Press, 2007.

Barbara G. Markway and Gregory P. Markway, *Painfully Shy: How to Overcome Social Anxiety and Reclaim Your Life.* New York: St. Martin's, 2001.

Reneau Peurifoy, *Anxiety, Phobias, and Panic.* New York: Warner, 2005.

Benjamin A. Root, *Understanding Panic and Other Anxiety Disorders.* Jackson, MS: University of Mississippi Press, 2000.

Jerilyn Ross and E. Claflin, *Triumph over Fear: A Book of Help and Hope for People with Anxiety, Panic Attacks, and Phobias.* New York: Bantam Doubleday Dell, 1998.

Allen Shawn, *Wish I Could Be There: Notes from a Phobic Life.* New York: Viking Penguin, 2007.

Murray B. Stein and John R. Walker, *Triumph over Shyness: Conquering Shyness and Social Anxiety.* New York: McGraw Hill, 2001.

Periodicals

Edgar Asher, "Freeing Troubled Minds," *Jerusalem Post*, March 23, 2007.

Carlos M. Coelho, Jorge A. Santos, Jorge Silverio, and Carles F. Silva, "Virtual Reality and Acrophobia: One-Year Follow-Up and Case Study," *CyberPsychology and Behavior*, June 2006.

A. De Jongh, "Treatment of Specific Phobias with Eye Movement Desensitization and Reprocessing (EMDR): Protocol, Empirical Status, and Conceptual Issues," *Journal of Anxiety Disorders*, 1999.

Tommy Fernandez, "How Shyness Quashes Careers: Paralyzing Anxiety Marginalizes Workers in Dog-Eat-Dog City," *New York Business*, June 27, 2005.

Hilary Freeman, "Health Zone: Two Hours of Therapy Made Me Forget My Lifelong Fear of the Dentist's Chair," *London Mirror*, December 14, 2000.

Lina Gega, Isaac Marks, and David Mataix-Cols, "Computer-Aided CBT Self-Help for Anxiety and Depressive Disorders: Experience of a London Clinic and Future Directions," *Journal of Clinical Psychology*, February 2004.

Rachele Kanigel, "Mind over Everything: Hypnosis Is No Panacea—but It Can Alleviate Physical Pain as Well as Phobia-Induced Stress and Anxiety," *Natural Health*, March 2007.

Neville J. King, Peter Muris, and Thomas H. Ollendick, "Childhood Fears and Phobias: Assessment and Treatment," *Child and Adolescent Mental Health*, 2005.

Robert T. London, "Is Social Phobia a Disorder or Not?" *Clinical Psychiatric News*, February 2005.

———, "Treating Fearful Fliers," *Clinical Psychiatric News*, March 2005.

Management Today, "What's Your Problem?" July 1, 2007.

Peter Monaghan, "Real Fear, Virtually Overcome," *Chronicle of Higher Education*, October 15, 2004.

Michael J. Mufson, "Coping with Anxieties and Phobias," *Harvard Special Health Report*, July 2006.

——— "What Are Anxiety Disorders?" *Harvard Special Health Report*, July 2006.

Kim Ode, "High Anxiety: Bridge Phobia Crosses into World of Panic; Fear of Bridges Is Real, but It's More About Feeling Trapped than Fear That It Will Collapse. Experts Say Treatments Have a High Success Rate," *Minneapolis Star Tribune*, August 11, 2007.

Lies Ouwerkerk, "How Worried Are You About It? Is It Normal Anxiety or a Disorder?" *Recorder* (Sherbrooke, Quebec), March 27, 2007.

Jo Revill, "Scared of Spiders? Take This Pill: A Readily Available Anti-tuberculosis Drug Could Also Cure Man's Deepest Darkest Phobias," *London Observer*, November 30, 2003.

Sarah Simmonds, "Charlie's Problem with Dogs," *Therapy Today*, September 2006.

Shannon Sutherland, "How to Get Back in the Chair: Electric Cure for Phobics?" *National Posts* (Mills, Ontario), May 23, 2003.

Ria Voorhaar, "Terror Nullified? (Taxidevophobia Means Travel Phobia Which Is Due to Bombings)," *Traveltrade*, October 19, 2005.

INDEX